P9-AON-591

Teacher/Teachim
The Toughest Game in Town

I can live for two months
on a good compliment

Mark Twain

Teacher/Teachim

The Toughest Game in Town

Joel Macht

University of Denver

JOHN WILEY & SONS, INC.
New York · London · Sydney · Toronto

104157

Copyright © 1975, by John Wiley & Sons, Inc.

All rights reserved. Published simultaneously in Canada.

No part of this book may be reproduced by any means, nor
transmitted, nor translated into a machine language without the written permission of the publisher.

Library of Congress Cataloging in Publication Data:
Macht, Joel, 1938–
    Teacher/teachim.

    Bibliography: p.
    Includes index.
    1. Learning, Psychology of. I. Title.

LB1051.M19   371.1'02   75-2082
ISBN 0-471-56242-4
ISBN 0-471-56243-2 pbk.
Printed in the United States of America

10 9 8 7 6 5 4 3 2 1

To Eunice and Manny, Charlie and Bernice,
Sig and Bea, Morton and Sophia

My Most Important Teachers

To Dave Kaufman's Ha-Wa-Ya

The Finest "School" I Ever
Went To

ОД: -2

Contents

104157

If One
Is Lost...

"I hope you will excuse my bluntness, but you've got to be kidding!" Miss Martin exclaimed. "I mean, you really must be joking. I simply cannot do what you are asking. I am certain the others feel the same way. I have thirty-two students in my class, not just one or two. I'm lucky, some of the others have thirty-five. We do not have any help. We are by ourselves. Do you know what it is like to teach thirty students without any help?"

"I think I do," the speaker responded. "I never said teaching was an easy job."

"I know you never said it, but you are implying it. You are telling me that I *must* reach every child in my class and I am telling you, as honestly as I know how, that I can't do it. In fact, if I were to do everything you're suggesting, I wouldn't have time to reach half of them. I know you believe strongly in what you are saying, and I appreciate that. But you are not being practical. With my methods, I am at least getting through to most of the students."

"But most is not all," the speaker answered, "and most, perhaps, means that some are being lost. I know the system is rough. A thirty-to-one ratio is, at best, overwhelming and, at worst, close to being impossible. But I wonder how you and I select who that one is that is lost? He certainly belongs to someone. I wonder whether that someone would go along with our choice?" the speaker asked rhetorically.

The audience of fifty or so teachers was very quiet. After a few moments, a young teacher stood. All eyes in the room focused on her.

"There is more to this than just the ratio," the teacher began. "You are forgetting the obvious fact that some students simply cannot be taught. Some of them do not care. Some do not have the intellectual capacity to learn what is being presented. There will always be a couple of students who have emotional problems and learning disabilities. If we spend too much time with them we will shortchange the capable students. There will always be a couple of students who fail."

Again, silence returned to the auditorium. The speaker paused for a moment, looked down at his notes, then closed his folder. "I'm not certain where to begin. You have raised so many critical issues that I'm somewhat at a loss as to what to say."

"If you recall," he continued, "the purpose of this presentation was to present to you some ideas that have been considered and tried by many of your colleagues. I never said that the suggestions were the 'answers' to everything, or the cures to all your very real problems. All I suggested was that there are several things you can do to make your task a little easier. Ultimately, what you do with the suggestions is your choice. But you have a responsibility to your students—every one of them. You have the responsibility, the obligation, to help each one of your students attain a measure of success. If you negate that responsiblity, that obligation, you should get out of teaching right this minute. Every student must have the opportunity to experience success—or else *you* fail! I believe these ideas we have looked at will help your students gain that success."

"Are you suggesting responsibility to all at the expense of some?" Miss Martin questioned.

"No, not at all," the speaker quickly answered. "There is little question that some students learn more rapidly than others. Some students come into our classes with a great deal of background material, which facilitates our job as teachers. Some students already know how to learn, while others have to learn how to learn. Your responsibility is to determine what differences the students bring into your class and then to design, as best you can, a program or approach that best fits the individual student. Your responsibility, as I see it, is to keep the educational door open for each of your students. This means that if you find that you are not succeeding with a particular student, you must try to provide some alternatives so that he still has the opportunity to experience the previously mentioned success."

"Are you suggesting an individually designed program for each student?" another teacher asked.

"Yes, unless you are fortunate enough to have two or more students who bring to your classroom the *exact* same amount of information; the *exact* same skills in learning how to learn; the *exact* same interest in your subject matter; and the *exact* same amount of drive, desire, motivation, whatever you wish to call it, to make the effort to succeed," responded the speaker.

"You are talking about Utopia!" Miss Martin exclaimed.

"No, I am talking about a challenge. I am talking about an educational Hippocratic oath, a statement offered to each one of your students that you will, to the best of your ability, do everything that you can to help him succeed," the speaker answered.

"Will you agree that some students will not be able to succeed?" someone asked from the back of the auditorium.

"Succeed at what?"

"Let's just say succeed at obtaining success," the same voice answered.

"No! I will not agree with that," the speaker retorted.

"Are you saying that every single student can experience success?" another asked.

"I can say nothing else but that. In fact, I have to say that every single student *must* experience some success," the speaker continued.

"That's a heavy burden you are placing on us," still another teacher commented.

"You're in a heavy profession," the speaker responded.

My
Boundaries

What you are about to read is not a textbook; it is a "talkbook." It is a book that will talk with you about things related to your profession. Unfortunately, this book will not make you a great teacher. Your professor will be able to give you several very good reasons why that is the case. This book will not attempt to answer or even discuss the many problems being discussed in today's educational world. A 1000-page manuscript would still only touch the surface. Additionally, this book will not cure your many classroom difficulties. If you have ever taught before or observed teachers in action, you will know that no one book can ever accomplish such a noble goal.

But this book will help you a great deal. It will make your task as teacher, easier. It will increase your chances of positively influencing all the students in your class. It will help you help your students experience some success.

What You Do Matters

I am taking the position that you have (or will have) a tremendous amount of influence on what goes on in your classroom, perhaps more influence than you have ever imagined. Things *do* happen as a result of what you do. As such, I am going to concentrate on your behavior, what you do and how it affects what your students will do. Not a very dramatic theme? As I am certain you know, there is a lot of talk these days about *your* accountability as a teacher. Parents want to know how a teacher is influencing their child. Is he or she helping or, perhaps, accidentally hindering the youngster's progress? Teachers, good teachers, also want to know the answer to the same question.

The sad truth is, however, that some teachers won't even ask themselves the question. They have found that it is much easier and *safer* to avoid the issue altogether. But, if you have the courage (and I mean just that) to look at yourself, to keep tabs on your own behavior, to hold yourself accountable to *yourself,* and to accept the praise for the helping as well as the responsibility for the hindering, I believe you will have taken a giant step toward professionalism and honesty. Equally as important, you will have taken a step *for* your students.

Exactly the Opposite

Sometimes our reactions to students' behavior results in exactly the opposite of what we wished might happen. For example, we might set out to help a student try to refrain from a behavior that is annoying to the entire class. Without us realizing it, our reactions to his behavior may actually *increase* his disturbing activities. Although we do not mean for this to happen, it nevertheless does. It is very important, therefore, to be aware of how we affect our students' behavior since our actions may not affect the student as we intended.

A Taste of His Own Medicine

One of my former students, who was presently doing her student teaching, came to me with the following account of something she had observed while working in her assigned classroom.

A fourth-grade boy had developed the habit of occasionally walking around his room administering unwelcomed "knuckle burns" (rubbing his knuckles on the top of one of his fellow student's head) whenever he felt the time was right. Having seen this several times, his teacher decided to give him a taste of his own medicine. Each time she observed the youngster perform his little game, she immediately went to him and calmly showed him what he had just done. His own head was the location of the teacher's demonstration. As far as the teacher was concerned, the problem was solved. The student teacher, however, did not share her optimism. She told me that from a humanitarian standpoint, there had to be a better way to handle the situation. She also expressed concern over the fact that the teacher had failed to find out what effect her reaction had on the student's knuckle burning. When she mentioned this latter point to the teacher, she was told that the youngster was "surely doing it less often."

Unfortunately, the student teacher had not kept track of the number of times the student played his game prior to the teacher's intervention. Therefore, she had no way of really knowing wether the teacher's estimate of "less often" was correct. Nevertheless, clandestinely, the student teacher began to keep a count of the student's behavior for a period of five days.

What Do You Suppose She Found?

For the first three days of her observation, the student played his game an average of three times during a one-hour period. By the fifth day, his game playing almost doubled. Believe it or not, six of his fellow students were the recipients of a set of knuckles not so gently rubbed on the tops of their heads. One might cautiously conclude that the teacher's approach was not bringing about her desired end—the reduction of the knuckle burning.

It was suggested that the student teacher talk with her teacher about the "findings." Fortunately for everyone, the astonished teacher, once having seen the records, decided that her approach was not working and that a new one needed to be considered.

Of course, there is no guarantee that the teacher's second approach would be any more humane or successful than her first. But we can hope that her experience with the above situation has taught her that it is important to see what effect her approach is having on her students. Instead of simply trying something and leaving it at that, it is critical to find out what *is* happening as a result of the trying.

They Are Either Very Nearsighted or They're Sleeping

Mrs. Hay held the distinction of being the oldest teacher in the town's only elementary school. She was always fond of telling her pupils that she had taught many of their mothers and fathers. It was generally conceded by the other members of the teaching staff that Mrs. Hay always had the most well-behaved classes. She never seemed to have a discipline problem. The children were "always" quiet, respectful, and courteous.

There was, however, a very curious thing about Mrs. Hay's classes. The principal always had a devil of a time finding a substitute teacher for the class when Mrs. Hay was away from school. Apparently, any substitute teacher would be "raked over the coals" by Mrs. Hay's quiet, respectful, courteous pupils, and the money for substituting was not enough to compensate for the "raking."

The principal had only been at the school for two months. He had been so busy adjusting to his new surroundings that he had spent very little time observing "his" teachers in action. However, after the third substitute teacher had politely refused to take over Mrs. Hay's class, he decided to set aside his paperwork and quietly observe Mrs. Hay's reading class.

The door to the class was barely open. Mrs. Hay noticed him immediately as soon as he stepped in and she smiled and nodded her recognition. The principal quickly moved to the back of the classroom to avoid disturbing the twenty-eight second graders. The stories he had heard about Mrs. Hay's quiet children were evidently true. Not only were the children quiet, they appeared to be asleep. Each child had his head firmly planted on the top of his desk. He noticed that the only signs of life in the room were the shallow breathing of the youngsters and the rapid pacing of Mrs. Hay as she walked up and down each aisle, peering down at the pupils. He sat in the back of the room observing the "reading" class for approximately five minutes. Finally, the quietness got to him and he walked toward the classroom door. Once again, Mrs. Hay smiled and nodded his departure. Dumbly, he walked back to his office. "What in the world is going on?" he thought to himself.

During her break, Mrs. Hay was summoned to the principal's office. As she later recalled, it was the first time any of the six principals she had worked under had ever requested her presence.

"That was a reading class I observed, wasn't it?" the principal asked.

"The 10:05 class, yes, that's one of my reading groups."

"May I ask you what was going on?" queried the principal.

"Reading, of course," Mrs. Hay responded indignantly.

"Oh yes, I'm certain of that, but I was referring to the students having their heads down on their desks."

"They were all being punished."

"What did they *all* do?" the principal asked in disbelief.

"I have a rule and the children know it. When any one of the children fail to do their reading assignments, they all must put their heads on their desks for twenty full minutes, and they must be quiet," she quickly added.

"May I ask you what good your 'punishment' does?"

"It teaches the children to do their work, to be quiet, respectful, and courteous. I have been doing it this way," Mrs. Hay continued, "for more than thirty-five years. My children are *always* very quiet, respectful, and courteous."

"Don't you think you might come up with a better way to help the youngsters learn their assignments? After all, isn't it pretty difficult to read when your head is on your desk?"

"First of all, I do not appreciate your humor. Second of all, my method works," Mrs. Hay said.

"I assume by that, you mean your students do their assignments?"

"That is precisely what I mean," Mrs. Hay responded curtly.

"How many times have you 'punished' them this week?" the principal asked.

"Three times, at the most, I think. My pupils know what happens when they fail to do their work."

"Yes, I am certain of that," the principal answered without hesitation. "They get to rest up for their gym period the following hour," he said to himself.

Mrs. Hay's method did "work." It did something. It did influence the pupils' behavior. But what was the outcome of her influence? What happened to the youngsters' behavior as a result of her approach? What happened to their reading skills? What happened to their ideas about school? What had Mrs. Hay actually done? I doubt she had any idea as to what was actually happening. Yet there is a good chance that she will continue with her methods. There is also an equally good chance that her present and future students will continue to rake and rest. Mrs. Hay enjoyed the "secure" life of an ostrich!

A Moment to Look

Since our students are the ones who ultimately lose out as a result of our unintentional influencing, it behooves us, for their sake, to take a moment or two to look at what we are doing. We may, of course, be pleasantly surpised to discover that things are going well, or we may see that something needs to be changed. The "seeing" is critical because, if change is indicated, we must make it. The stakes are too high to do otherwise. H. G. Wells once said, "Human history becomes more and more a race between education and catastrophe." "Ostriches" will cause that race to be lost—then we all lose.

Social Behaviors and the Classroom Teacher

The First Step Toward Accountability

"Has there been any change in Billy's behavior?" Mother asked.

"It seems to me that he is more comfortable in class and that he feels better about being here," the teacher responded.

"I am certainly glad to hear that. His father and I were becoming a little worried. How about his class work?"

"There has been noticeable improvement in his reading and math. Let me show you these charts. What I do is keep a record of each student's performance in class, particularly in the areas of reading and math, so that I can show the parents how their children are doing. Notice that Billy's vocabulary has jumped by about forty words. He is making fewer mistakes when he reads. His chart shows that he made only three mistakes during his last reading assignment. That's tremendous improvement. He was making as many as ten mistakes on the same amount of work. Also, something that I am very pleased to see. He seems to have conquered his regrouping problem in subtraction—not one mistake on his last three exercises. That is very good," the teacher proclaimed.

"Thanks for all your help," Mother said. "You certainly make it easy for us to know how our son is doing. Please keep in touch with us about the other problem."

"You mean his feeling comfortable in the classroom?" the teacher asked.

"Yes."

"As you probably know, that is a little more difficult to keep track of," the teacher answered, "but I will certainly keep you informed as best I can."

Seeing Is Believing

Next time you are in a classroom, whether you are the teacher or one of the students, take a few moments to look around the room. Don't look for anything special. Instead, just watch what some of the other people are *doing.* Without much effort, you will see many different forms of behavior. Some of the students will be sitting quietly. Others will be talking with a friend. There may be a few who are writing, a few who are sleeping, and a few who are looking at what you are doing. Regardless of what is actually going on, each and every person in your room is behaving in some way or another.

FIRST YOUDOIT[1]

Take a minute to count and jot down the number of people who are sitting quietly, writing, looking at a book, talking, or standing.

Behavior

	Sitting Quietly	Writing	Looking at a Book	Talking	Standing
Number of people					

Simple task, wasn't it? All you had to do was to look for the occurrence of the particular behavior and then make a mark in the appropriate block. Now, try this next task.

SECOND YOUDOIT

Look around the room. Count and jot down the number of people who are feeling sad, happy, angry, or who aren't feeling anything.

---

*[1] A youdoit is something your professor and I would like you to do!

Behavior

	Feeling Sad	Feeling Happy	Feeling Angry	Aren't Feeling
Number of People				

If you are like me, you probably found this second task a little more difficult than the first. You may have found yourself saying, "Well, that guy over there looks sad, but he may be tired. That is why his face looks as it does." Or, "She is laughing, so I guess that means she is happy." Quickly see if you can find someone staring out the window. Ask yourself this question, "Is he daydreaming or is he thinking?" Pretty difficult to be certain, isn't it? You could, of course, ask him, but imagine the answer you would probably receive from a second grader who was suddenly asked by his teacher whether he was thinking or daydreaming.

Why these first two youdoits? Let's see.

HOW ARE YOU AND YOUR STUDENTS DOING?

Most people seem to enjoy the knowledge that they have successfully completed a task. When, for example, a newly baked cookie tastes good, the taste "tells" us that all the effort that went into its baking was worthwhile. Likewise, music instead of static lets the do-it-yourself repairman know that the time spent assembling his radio was well spent. Like the baker and repairman, teachers are no different. They, too, enjoy being "told" that they have had a hand in accomplishing something worthwhile. Unfortunately, they may never know what they have accomplished; unlike the pleasant taste and satisfying sound, the educational "end product" can be very elusive.

This absence of information is more important than it may seem at first. Without it, the teacher will have a most difficult time evaluating his program to see if he is helping or hindering his students. That, of course, could be disastrous, particularly if the hindering effect is occurring. Additionally, without the knowledge of how his students are doing, the teacher loses a major source of reinforcement for himself, particularly if the helping effect is taking place.

If, on the other hand, you have some type of observable end product on which you can make a progress-like statement, you will be better able to see what effect, if any, you are having. That is, again, critical.

AN OBSERVABLE END PRODUCT

An observable end product is some activity that can be seen or measured. For example, Billy's teacher and Mother were both interested in the youngster's progress in math, reading, and his feeling more comfortable. The teacher had little difficulty describing Billy's progress in math and reading. She had literally kept a record of the change or growth in these subject areas. As she indicated, however, being aware of the youngster's state of being comfortable was not quite as easy.

Certain activities are more observable than others. If you will quickly look at your first two youdoits, I think you will see what I mean. It is fairly simple to know whether a student is sitting, writing, or talking. They can be seen. On the other hand, notice how much more difficult it was for you to be certain that one of your fellow students was feeling sad.

WHAT DOES THE STUDENT HAVE TO DO IN ORDER FOR YOU TO KNOW?

If the only behaviors teachers were interested in were the easily observable ones, many of our problems would never occur. However, such is not the case. We are most assuredly interested in behaviors such as "thinking more clearly," "feeling more comfortable," and "being more creative." Many of us would like our students to experience these feelings and activities, and an equal number of us devote a good deal of our energy toward these goals.

Assume for the moment that I am correct in saying that it is easier to know whether a student is talking than it is to know that he is thinking more clearly.

THIRD YOUDOIT

Below I have listed several activities or behaviors that are often very difficult to observe. See if you can come up with a few ways to know that the activities are actually taking place.

1. Thinking more clearly.   a. _____

    _____

    _____

    _____

b. _____
_____
_____
_____

2. Feeling more comfortable.   a. _____
_____
_____
_____

b. _____
_____
_____
_____

3. Being more creative.   a. _____
_____
_____
_____
_____

b. _____
_____
_____
_____

If you found this task frustrating, welcome to the club. Many of us have a hard time with this assignment. Take a moment to look at what you wrote. Have you used some terms that, perhaps, will need some additional redefining? It usually happens that way. For example, if you said that you will know that a student is feeling more comfortable when he is "feeling less anxious," then without realizing it, you haven't progressed very far. How will you know when he is feeling less anxious? If you said that you will know that a student is thinking more clearly when he "uses his mind more effectively," then again, you are going to have to answer the question, "How will you know that he is using his mind more effectively?"

The problem is more than just semantics. The problem is that your answers are no more observable than what you were asked to describe. Let me see if I can help you a little. I will give you a hint. Think about it then try the task once again.

What does the student have to *DO* in order for you to know that he is (1) thinking more clearly; (2) feeling more comfortable; (3) being more creative? What must you observe from the student before you will know that these activities are actually taking place? What will you *LOOK* for; how must he *BEHAVE*; what should the student *DO*, before you will be certain that he, in fact, is doing what you desire?

FOURTH YOUDOIT

Activity		*Behavior*
1. Thinking more clearly.	a.	_____
		_____
	b.	_____
		_____
	c.	_____
		_____
2. Feeling more comfortable.	a.	_____
		_____
	b.	_____
		_____
	c.	_____
		_____

3. Being more creative. a. ———————————————

———————————————

b. ———————————————

———————————————

c. ———————————————

———————————————

Were you any more successful? When I am faced with the above task, I rely heavily on the hint. Let me offer you a few answers that some of my own students have come up with and see if you agree with any of them.

1. Thinking more clearly.
    a. Answering questions more accurately.
    b. Asking questions related to topic of discussion.
    c. Answering questions without a great delay.
    d. Offering suggestions to fellow students about their answers.

2. Feeling more comfortable.
    a. More social inter action with peers.
    b. Volunteering information in class.
    c. Less crying or whining in class (young student).
    d. Participating in class discussion.
    e. Smiling and laughing more often

3. Being more creative.
    a. Exploring available supplies and materials.

        b. Answering questions in
           ways not tried before.

        c. Putting things
           together differently.

(Notice that almost without exception, you and I would be able to see the above activities taking place.)

There are, of course, many other possible answers, and the longer you teach, the more answers you will come up with. For now, keep in mind that if you are going to set out to influence activities such as those described above, give yourself (and your students) a chance to know how effective you are. Define the activities so they are observable.

COMMUNICATING WITH ONE ANOTHER

There is another reason to concentrate on observable, well-defined types of behaviors. We need, to the best of our ability, to communicate with one another in ways which minimize misunderstanding and confusion. Because many of us have our own "unique" definitions for various terms, sometimes we communicate something that was unintended to a listener. For example, if I tell you that in one of my classes I have a student who is very disruptive, I may accidentally give you the impression that the student *does* certain things when he actually *doesn't*. For me, the term disruptive stands for various types of behaviors. The problem is that the term may not mean the same to you. If that be the case, we may be saying different things to one another without even realizing it. Try one more youdoit and see what you end up with.

FIFTH YOUDOIT

Below I have listed two words that are quite common. Without talking to one of your neighbors, write down what the terms mean to you—what the student probably *does*. After you have done so, compare your answers with one of your classmates.

Term	*What the Student Probably Does*
1. Disruptive	a. _____
	b. _____
	c. _____
2. Anxious	a. _____
	b. _____
	c. _____

There is a good possibility that you and your classmates did not agree on the exact description of what the disruptive or anxious student probably does. I think you can see that the more comparisons you make with your classmates, the greater the likelihood that confusion will exist. There is a very easy way to avoid this type of confusion. Initially, at least, simply describe what the student does instead of referring to him as disruptive or anxious. That way you will be talking about observable behaviors and not about labels that may mean different things to different people. Of course, once you and your classmates agree on a label, then your label will serve as a descriptive, shorthand notation for the agreed on behaviors. But remember, each time you talk with a new classmate or teacher, you are once again going to have to be cautious about misunderstanding.

I remember one of my professors who made the following statement: "People who are anxious are sometimes hostile." It took him the entire period to tell us what he meant. When he was finished many of us were still confused. After much wasted time he eventually told us what, *in his view,* "anxious" and "hostile" people *do*. That helped, but did not solve the problem. He then had to tell us how many times "sometimes" was. I believe he was quite sorry that he brought the whole thing up in the first place.

Resolution:
This Year
I Will Work
Above My
Maximum
Capacity

"This may not make any sense to you, Mrs. Jones, but the problem with your son is that he keeps working above his maximum capacity. If we could somehow teach him to work within himself, I know he would enjoy school much more than he does now," Jimmy's teacher advised.

"Excuse my ignorance," Mrs. Jones said, "but how is it possible for a child to work *above* his *maximum* capacity?"

"That is a difficult concept to understand. Most parents are confused by it," the teacher responded. "You see, your son's IQ is just barely 93, yet he keeps making straight A's. He shouldn't be doing that well."

"Do me a favor," Mrs. Jones pleaded, "please do not tell Jimmy that he's not supposed to be doing so well."

* * *

"This is not an unusual case. There are a lot of children like your daughter. I'm not supposed to do this, but let me show you something. Look at the figure on this line. The 133 indicates your daughter's IQ. It's obvious that a youngster with this much native ability should be tops in her class. But your daughter isn't."

"I thought she was doing pretty well," Mother quietly said.

"She's only making B's and there are many children with less intelligence who are doing much better than Debbie," the teacher responded.

"Is it possible that the IQ test was wrong?" Mother asked.

"I beg your pardon," remarked the teacher.

* * *

"I would suggest that you and your husband get used to the idea that your son simply does not have the ability to do better than average work."

"Who says so?" Father asked in a stern voice.

"His tests say so," the teacher politely responded.

"He was doing a lot better than average work before he entered this class," Father retorted.

"Well, that just means that your son is really an overachiever," the teacher explained.

"That's funny," Mother said, "last year one of the teachers told us he was an underachiever."

"That may have been true last year, but not this year," the teacher offered.

"I'm confused," Mother admitted.

"So is she," Father quietly said to his wife.

* * *

The above conversations are not real. They are exaggerations. What is real, however, is that education has provided teachers with various means that actually close educational doors instead of keeping them open when used incorrectly. As Don Bushell, Jr. describes in his excellent text, *Classroom Behavior—A Little Book for Teachers:*

> "There are a number of educational practices which no matter how noble their intentions, have turned out to be 'excuses not to teach.' " (p.5)

Dr. Bushell's statement is dramatic and could be labeled controversial. But his view is one that you and I should consider carefully. Very shortly we will be looking at ways to bring about changes in students' academic and social behavior. A teacher's task is tough enough as it is, and some of the practices to which Bushell refers are obstacles best removed before we go any further.

WHAT YOU EXPECT MAY BE WHAT YOU GET

From the preface to *Pygmalion in the Classroom,* written by Robert Rosenthal and Lenore Jacobson:

> "When we are led to expect that we are about to meet a pleasant person, our treatment of him at first meeting may, in fact, make him a more pleasant person. If we are led to expect that we shall encounter an unpleasant person, we may approach him so defensively that we make him into an unpleasant person." (p. vii)

Would it surprise you to know that there is a reasonably good chance that the expectations that you have about one of your students may have an effect on that student's behavior? Some fascinating research by the above mentioned authors suggests just that. Assuming the authors' data stand up under further investigation, it may be accurate to suggest that some of your students will be affected not so much by what they do, but by what you expect them to do.

Suppose, for example, that you find out, by looking at previous reports and listening to other teachers, that one of the students in your class comes from a depressed, low-socioeconomic area and you conclude, therefore, that the student will not be one of your best students. On the other hand, another of the students comes from a well-to-do area and the youngster's father is a famous physician. You might guess that this second student "because of his background" will perform very well in your class. Your expectations of these students will likely influence the way you respond to them, and they may (although still problematical) perform as you *predicted,* regardless of their actual skills.

> "Twenty percent of the children in a certain elementary school were reported to their teachers as showing unusual potential for intellectual growth. The names of these 20 percent of the children were drawn by means of a table of random numbers, which is to say that the names were drawn out of a hat. Eight months later these unusual or 'magic' children showed significantly greater gains in IQ than did the remaining children who had not been singled out for teachers' attention." (From *Pygmalion in the Classroom, p.vii)*

From wizardry we move to Dean Arthur P. Coladarci's ornithology, as he writes:

> "Consider the following pedagogical parable. Mrs. Jones, school teacher, is expecting a list of her new fifth grade pupils with the IQ's for each contained thereon—which she will use to make ability groupings ('Ravens,' 'Robins,' and 'Bluebirds,' of course). She receives, at that moment, a list of her new pupils with the locker numbers assigned to each. Unfortunately, this list is untitled and she assumes that she has the IQ's she has been waiting for. Mrs. Jones makes her three groups, assigning children with low locker numbers to the 'Ravens,' high locker-numbered pupils go to the 'Bluebirds,' and the 'Robins' comprise those children with locker numbers in the 95-110 range. She then proceeds to 'enrich' and 'challenge' the 'Bluebirds,' hold 'average expectations' for the 'Robins,' and 'protect' and 'non-frustrate' the 'ravens.' And, lo and behold, the groupings 'prove' to be correct—at the end of the first semester, the Ravens have made less progress than the Bluebirds!" (Coladarci, 1966)

The potential effect of your expectations regarding your students is something that you, hopefully, will keep in mind. Don't be mislead into believing that a child will not perform well simply because someone suggests that to you. If you expect that Johnny will be the most disruptive student in your class, he may just be that, and for reasons already suggested. If you are told that Mary has only borderline intelligence, or that she will "always" be a C student, give her a chance. Don't close the door on her by treating her as if the offered information is the final answer. Be more concerned about your teaching skills and the educational environment you provide for her.

HOW MUCH CAN A STUDENT LEARN?

The simple truth is that we do not know how much any given child can learn. Yet, despite information to the contrary, teachers often place arbitrary limitations on students. Given this fact and given the previously discussed "Pygamalion" effect, I think you can see what the outcomes of these set limitations might be. From *Changing Classroom Behavior: A Manual for Precision Teaching* by Merle Meacham and Allen Wiesen:

"Unfortunately, teachers. . .may set imaginary limits on students. If they consider a child bright, they may spare no effort to ensure that he is provided an enriched classroom environment. On the other hand, if they consider a child dull, they assume that he is incapable of progressing much, despite the environment, and expect only minimal learning. . .we are not yet capable of predicting how much children are able to learn, and certainly not yet ready to pinpoint the limits of the individual child. . .if a child is presumed to be 'slow' and is consequently placed in a low level environment, he will very likely learn at a low level. To then assume that it is the child's native inability to learn that is responsible is overlooking the obvious." (p.7)

You must make the assumption that each and every child can learn. How much, we do not know. How fast, we do not know. But limitations such as "slow learner" and "borderline ability" are often invented prophecies that too frequently come true. And the door closes just a little more.

INTELLIGENCE TESTS

Dr. Robert M. Smith, from his book, *Teacher Diagnosis of Educational Difficulties:*

"Conventional intelligence tests: CANNOT reveal the capacity or potential of a student.

Conventional intelligence tests: CAN provide fair predictions of school success, assuming we do nothing exceptional to help or hinder certain students and thus destroy the prediction." (p. 45)

(If Dr. Smith's last statement did not "grab" you, read it once more!)

If you are told that a student has an IQ of 133, what would you expect from him? How about the student with a measured IQ of 55? If you let them, both scores *will* affect you. You will make predictions; you will have expectations; you will make assumptions, and all of these will affect how you might otherwise react to the student.

Understand that you can learn things from IQ scores. For example, assuming that the test scores were validly obtained, they can tell you where a youngster stands in reference to the norm group on which the test was established. But this does not necessarily mean that the youngster will always remain at the statistical location. There is a better than excellent chance that you can change his position as a result of what you do in your classroom. IQ scores can also tell you, depending on the type of test, some of the experiences the child has had prior to taking the test. But that surely doesn't mean that those will be the only experiences he is going to encounter. As the child's teacher, you are going to influence him; you are going to introduce him to many new experiences. Certain IQ tests can give you some information regarding the student's present verbal skills, such as vocabulary. But, again, there is a better than excellent chance that each day you talk with him you are going to increase that component of his intelligence quotient.

The point is that a child's IQ is changeable! Hayne Reese and Lewis Lipsitt (1970) point that out succinctly.

"An IQ is not a fixed attribute of an individual in the way that blood type is. It is. . .a score on a test. As such, it is subject to change from a variety of influences. . ."

One of the major ideas of the book you are now reading is that *you are one of those "variety of influences."*

READINESS

As Bushell indicates (1973), "Perhaps the most ubiquitous of all excuses not to teach, particularly in primary grades, is the concept of readiness." (p.8)

Which One is READy

Mrs. Lard believes that children will read when they are ready. She waits for her pupils to demonstrate their readiness before reading exercises are begun. In her class of twenty-seven children, some are reading, and are, therefore, ready to read. Some are not reading and are, therefore, not ready to read. When asked how she knows that the latter group is not ready, she tells us that she has presented them with reading material, but they have failed to show any interest. She further tells us that she will wait for them to indicate their interest before she pursues the area of reading with them.

(Let's look at the backgrounds of three of the youngsters *before* they entered Mrs. Lard's classroom.)

Jack: Like the others, Jack is seven years of age. His father is a librarian. His mother is a lawyer. He is an only child. Both Mother and Father are avid readers—books, magazines, and newspapers. Their work schedules allow them to be home at five o'clock in the evening. After dinner Mother and Father usually read something. In many instances, Jack can be found sitting by his parents, looking intently at what is being read. On occasion, while reading *Good Housekeeping*, Mother shows Jack how various letters, when put together, make words. Every once in awhile, Jack repeats the word Mother presented to him. Mother and Father demonstrate how proud they are of their young son.

Mary: Mary has three brothers and a newborn sister. Father is a dock worker, and he works the evening shift most of the time. With the exception of Sundays, he rarely has an opportunity to eat with his children. Mother's day is spent taking care of the children, the house, and her husband. When the children are finally in bed, she spends her remaining waking hours unwinding. The television is on in Mary's house from 7:00 a.m. to 9:00 p.m. It is turned off only after the children are asleep. When Mother is not too tired, she will read some of the new recipes found in *Family Circle*. Although there are magazines and books in Mary's house, they usually stay on the bookshelf.

Jamie: Jamie's father died when he was very young. He has four older sisters and one older brother. His mother is on welfare, and all her energy is spent attempting to provide a stable home (and meals) for her family. Mother was forced to quit school during sixth grade so she could get a job to help her mom and dad. With the exception of supermarket specials in the newspaper, Jamie's mother has not read anything for enjoyment or interest in ten years. Her reading skills are very weak, and her general knowledge is limited. Academic success is not particularly important to her or her children.

Question. Which child will be "ready" first? Second? Third?

Question. Has the home environment had anything to do with the youngsters' "readiness"?

Question. Assuming the home environment does not change very much, which of the children will be reading last, if ever?

Question. Can the teacher do something about the situation instead of waiting for interest to be shown?

Question. At what age would you expect Jamie to demonstrate reading readiness if he continues to experience no encouragement from his mother, no encouragement from his teacher, and no success from his slightest attempts at reading—such as looking in the direction of a book?

There is no argument with the appropriate use of the term "readiness." A child, for example, will not walk at least until he has reached a sufficient state of physiological readiness. Once that state has been reached, the environment, almost without exception, provides him with many reasons to walk, and the youngster does so. Likewise, a young child will not be able to draw and write letters until he has reached a sufficient degree of physiological development. Prior to that time, drawing and writing will not be observed, despite attempts to bring them about.

When teachers use the term readiness, however, they are rarely talking about physiological development. Instead, they talk about "interest readiness," where the child shows no interest in a subject or activity, or "prerequisite readiness," where the youngster does not demonstrate the necessary skills to accomplish a particular activity. These are the types of "readiness" that have to be looked at carefully.

At best, it is highly questionable to assume that a child is not ready to become involved in an academic activity at the primary school level simply because the youngster has failed to indicate any interest or has failed to demonstrate a degree of success with the activity. If the environment so chooses, the interest level can be embellished by making the activity extremely inviting, thereby increasing the chances that the child will explore the available activity. And, if it so chooses, the environment can take the activity and reduce its level of difficulty to the point at which the child *demonstrates* the necessary prerequisite skills, which now increases the chances that the child will experience at least a measure of success.

Of course, the option is always available, in place of attempting to heighten interest or reduce complexity, to simply conclude that the child, indeed, is not ready. That is one of those "that settles that" kind of ostrich options.

In the provided examples, Jack is ready to read, in part, because of the way his environment has responded to him. Jamie, on the other hand, is *not* ready to pick up a book and read the opening paragraph because of what his environment has *not* done for him. But he *is* most certainly ready to be introduced to magazines, books, letters, words, pictures, and the like. Most two-year olds are at that stage of readiness,

104157

aren't they? From the information described, wouldn't you be interested in seeing if Jamie could do as well?

Final question.   Would Jack be as "ready" if he was raised in Jamie's family? Would Jamie be as far behind in "readiness" had he been brought up with Jack's parents?

The environment has a great deal to do with children's "readiness." A teacher, as a member of each child's school environment, can help—if he or she chooses to do so.

Despite Our Uniqueness, We Are Very Much the Same

All teachers, those who have taught in the past, those who are teaching today, and those who will teach tomorrow, have much in common.

KEY: By our actions we influence both the academic and social behavior of our students.

Regardless of our teaching philosophies, regardless of the location where our teaching takes place, and regardless of the types of students we work with, we all interact with students, and we all influence students.

When you have the chance, I would like you to make a visit to as many elementary schools and junior and senior high schools as possible. Try to observe as many different teachers as your time will allow. If you'll look carefully, you will notice something very interesting about all these different teachers. By watching what these teachers do, you will see that they are all attempting to influence their students' behavior. Do not be particularly concerned for now, at least, with what they say they *intend* to do, or *are going* to do, but concentrate on what they *do*.

I am so sure that we all have much in common that I am going to offer you some predictions about what you will hear and see. Although their words may differ slightly, the teachers' reactions will be very similar to many of the following.

"Billy, you did beautifully. I am very pleased with your work."

"Mary, will you please raise your hand before calling out."

"John, since you failed to turn in your assignment, you will miss recess today."

"Jack, your answer was perfect. I hope you will continue to keep up the good work."

"Debbie, you haven't progressed very far in your reading. We are going to change that, aren't we?"

"Mike, I am not going to put up with your antics any longer. I've already told you enough times. I will not tell you again."

"Ed, how many times have I told you to sit down? Now, sit down!"

SIXTH YOUDOIT

When you visit the schools, try to watch one particular child for about an hour. Look for an observable behavior that is occurring fairly frequently. Take a piece of paper and write down the precise description of the child's "target" behavior. Then mark down the number of times the behavior occurs and also mark down how the teacher responds (if he does) to *each* occurrence of the behavior. You can make a simple code to help you keep track of the teacher's reactions. You might also record *your* impressions during this observation period to discuss your findings with your classmates later.

Example

Child's Behavior

   a. *Out* of chair.
   b. Sitting *in* chair.

Teacher's Response and Code

   a. Praised the child (P)
   b. Yelled or warned
      the child (Y)
   c. No response (N)

Behavior

Child	Out of Chair			In Chair	
Child	1	1	1	1	1
Teacher	N*	Y	Y	N	N

1= one incident of behavior.

N*= teacher's reaction to the behavior. (See code)

Total. During a one-hour period in math class, the child left his seat three times and returned to his chair twice. The child received two warnings and one "no response" when he left his chair. The teacher did not respond to him (two "no responses") either time he returned to his chair. At the end of class, he was still walking around.

Observer Impressions. It almost seemed as if the child enjoyed being told to sit down. That's the way it looked to me. (That does sound crazy, doesn't it? Maybe I am wrong.)

WATCH FOR TWO THINGS

Arrange with your professor for a few moments of class time to discuss what several of you found during your sixth youdoit. Select a volunteer to record what was observed at each of the schools. On one side of the blackboard write down what behavior was observed, and across from the behavior write down how the teacher responded to the behavior.

What you will quickly observe is that each behavior resulted in (or was followed by) some action on the part of the teacher. (If one of your classmates indicates that the child's "target" behavior was reacted to by some of his peers as well as by the teacher, write down the peer reaction also.) Once you have a good sample of observations, sit back and look carefully at what has been written.

KEY: | When a student's behavior is closely followed by a reaction from his immediate environment, the student's future behavior may be affected.

Since all teachers, at one time or another, respond to the behaviors of each and every student, we can say that all of us have a potentially powerful effect on how our students will behave, what they will learn, and how they will feel toward school.

The Most Accurate Barometer

It is one thing to know that you do influence behavior. It is another thing to know how to determine the kind of effect you are having. As you will now see, your students' actual behavior will help you make this determination.

Scene

You are observing a third-grade history class. The teacher is asking questions about the previous day's reading assignment. She makes the following request of her students. "When I ask a question, please raise your hand if you feel you know the answer. Even if you aren't 100 percent certain of your answer, try anyway. But please do not call out your answer. That way, everyone will have an equal chance to participate."

As soon as the teacher asks her first question, most of the students raise their hands. One youngster is called on, and his answer is correct. The teacher thanks him for his answer and for raising his hand. Several more questions are asked and, in each case, the teacher selects one of the children whose hand was raised. However, on the next question, one of the students, in his excitement to participate, does not raise his hand. Instead, he loudly informs the teacher that he has the answer.

Instead of noticing that student, the teacher selects a young girl who is sitting next to him. The teacher says, "Mary, thank you for raising your hand. What do you think the answer is?" As soon as the young girl gave her answer, she was praised for her effort. On the very next question, the student who had called out just previously raised his hand. The teacher immediately asked him for his answer. When he finished, the teacher thanked him for raising his hand, and she told him that his answer was just fine. Thereafter, each student raised his hand, and all the students had an opportunity to show what they had read.

Teacher's goal: Each child should raise his hand when wishing to answer a question.

SEVENTH YOUDOIT

Answer the following questions.

1. What was the desired behavior the teacher wanted?

_____

2. How did the teacher respond to the desired behavior? (two answers)

a. _____

_____

b. _____

_____

3. What was the undesired behavior the teacher did not want?

_____

4. How did the teacher respond to the undesired behavior? (one answer)

a. _____

_____

5. Did the teacher reach her intended goal?

      yes   no

6. How would the *teacher* know whether her goal was accomplished?

_____

_____

KEY: | The *student's behavior* is the most accurate barometer a teacher has to determine what effect she is having on what they do.

Did the above teacher bring about the type of behavior she was interested in? If your answer is yes, then she accomplished what she intended. If your answer is no, then the teacher did not reach her intended goal. Let's compare answers.

1. What was the desired behavior the teacher wanted?

   Answer. She wanted the children to raise their hands when they wished to answer a question.

2. How did the teacher respond to the desired behavior?

   Answer.
   a. She called on the students when their hands were raised.
   b. She thanked them for raising their hands.

3. What was the undesired behavior the teacher did not want?

   Answer. She wanted the children to avoid calling out their answers.

4. How did the teacher respond to the undesired behavior?

   Answer. She did not respond to the students when they did not raise their hands.

5. Did the teacher reach her intended goal?

   Answer. Based on the information I provided, the answer appears to be *yes*.

6. How would the *teacher* know whether her goal was accomplished?

Answer. By watching her students' behavior. If they raised their hands, her goal was accomplished and her approach was working.

Try another example.

Scene

You are observing a seventh-grade science class. Each day the teacher provides a brand new experiment to make his class interesting and to make the present topic of discussion as clear as possible. He has explained to his students that many of the experiments are complicated and that it is necessary for the students to come to class on time. In that way, they will not miss any of the demonstration and he will not have to repeat any important information.

You have noticed that for the last three days, one particular student has come to class about ten minutes late. In each instance, the teacher has stopped his presentation when the latecomer walks into the room. The teacher, obviously upset, calls the youngster to the front of the room. For several minutes, he expresses his displeasure to the student and warns him that if his late behavior continues, he will be forced to take drastic action. After the explanation, the student is told to take his seat and not to disturb the class again.

You observe that when the student takes his seat, numerous smiles and gestures take place between the tardy student and several of his classmates.

Over the next ten days, you notice that the student is late to class seven times, and the teacher repeats his warning and demonstration of displeasure each of those seven days. On the three days that the youngster arrives on time, the teacher immediately begins his presentation and continues without comment to the student.

Teacher's goal: Each student should be in his seat on time.

EIGHTH YOUDOIT

Answer the following questions.
1. What was the desired behavior the teacher wanted?

2. How did the teacher respond to the desired behavior? (one answer)

_____

3. What was the undesired behavior the teacher did not want?

_____

4. How did the teacher respond to the undesired behavior? (probably two or three answers)

a. _____

b. _____

c. _____

5. Did the teacher reach his intended goal?

     yes   no

6. How would the teacher know whether his goal was accomplished?

_____

Let's compare again.

1. *Answer.* The teacher wanted each student to be in his seat on time.

2. *Answer.* He neglected to do anything, other than continue his presentation, when the student finally arrived on time.

3. *Answer.* The teacher did not want any of his students to be late.

4. *Answer.*
   a. He called the student to the front of the room.
   b. He expressed his displeasure for several minutes.
   c. He made repeated warnings and threats of drastic action.
      Optional fourth answer.
   d. The tardy student received a good deal of attention from some of his peers.

5. *Answer*. Almost, but not quite.
6. *Answer*. Again, by watching the behavior of *all* his students. The teacher should realized that his approach is not working as he intended because of the behavior of the one tardy student. The student's behavior, therefore, should tell the teacher that he needs to reevaluate his approach if he wishes to reach his goal.

One last quickie. As you will see, the questions to be answered will be slightly different than the two previous examples. Think about three things as you read the scene. First, what is the teacher trying to accomplish? Second, what is she *doing* to reach her objectives? Third, how are the students *affected by* the teacher's approach?

Scene

You are observing a second-grade math class. The teacher is having difficulty getting the children to do their workbook assignments in class. Believing that it is important for the youngsters to learn the concepts presented in the book, she decides to try the following program.

As soon as a student correctly completes one page of his workbook, the teacher will place one gold star by the student's name located on a chart placed in the front of the room. If a student fails to complete at least one half page of the workbook in the allotted time, the student will have to take his unfinished work and sit in the hallway until he has completed the full page. This will mean that the youngster will miss part of his free-time period, which is spent in the school library.

After three days of the new program, you see that all the students, minus two, are doing very well. These two continually fail to complete even one half page. For the next five days, the two "mavericks" can be found in the hallway instead of in the library. Over the next few weeks, fewer and fewer students are doing their math work and more and more of them are finding themselves sitting in the hallway.

Teacher's goal: To have each student compete one full page of their workbook during the allotted class time.

Any question about whether the teacher's goal was attained? Obviously, something is wrong. She ended up with a situation that was unintended. Do you have any ideas as to what might be responsible for the teacher's difficulties? Try this next youdoit.[2] I will ask you to come back to it shortly.

NINTH YOUDOIT

Answer the following questions.

1. What would be your reaction to the teacher about her telling you that gold stars *are* reinforcers (or rewards) for her youngsters?

   a. _____

   _____

   _____

   _____

   _____

2. What would be your reaction to the teacher about her telling you that sitting in the hallway *is* a form of punishment for her students?

   a. _____

   _____

   _____

   _____

   _____

3. What would be your reaction to the teacher about her telling you that going to the library *is* reinforcing to her students, while missing the opportunity to do the same *is* a form of punishment?

   a. _____

   _____

   _____

   _____

   _____

[2] Suggested answers are located in the youdoit section, p. 308.

4. Assuming that the teacher has failed to keep careful records of the students' previous math work, is there anything wrong with requiring that *all* the children complete at least one half page of their workbook, or one full page, prior to receiving a gold star?

a._____

_____

_____

_____

_____

_____

_____

_____

_____

_____

Behavior
Pairs

Up to this point, we have discussed the following.

1. Things do happen as a result of what teachers do.
2. What may happen in our classroom may not be what we had intended to happen.
3. We stand a much better chance of knowing what *is* happening if the behaviors we work with are observable.
4. Our students' demonstrated observable behavior is the most accurate barometer we have to determine how we *are* influencing what they do.

Now we will look at an idea that will lead us into the various approaches for bringing about changes in our students' behavior. As you will see, this idea will be with us for the remainder of this book.

YOUR STUDENTS' CLASSROOM BEHAVIOR

Have you ever considered the types of things you would like your students to do while in your classroom? Although this question may seem premature, you might begin to consider the types of behavior you are going to try to influence. Think about behaviors which, in your view, are most compatible with learning, exploration, problem solving, relevancy, a student's own personal interests, and so forth. If you experience some difficulty in developing ideas, watch the teachers from the various schools where you are observing. Ask them what they consider appropriate behaviors for their classroom objectives. Do not be concerned if you find that teachers have differing opinions as to what an appropriate behavior is, or which behavior is most likely to lead to a specific classroom objective. Not only do we differ with each other, we also find ourselves changing our own opinions regarding these behaviors.

WHAT TO DO AND WHAT NOT TO DO

Although I have made the following point before, I would like to call it to your attention again. Regardless of the preferences each of us have, regardless of the subject areas for which we are responsible, and regardless of the approach we take with and for our students, we all work with student behaviors. In fact, we all work with what I call sets of behaviors or behavior pairs. A behavior pair consists of two behaviors. The two behaviors, in many cases, are directly opposite. They are, so to speak, incompatible. The two behaviors cannot take place at the same time. For example, a student cannot be sitting in his chair and walking around the room at precisely the same time. He cannot run in the school hallway and walk in the hallway at the same time. He cannot be late and on time to class simultaneously.

TENTH YOUDOIT

While doing your observation at the various schools, watch for and record many different types of observable behaviors. Once you have listed five or ten such behaviors, develop an incompatible behavior to the ones you have just observed. Take a few moments in your class to compare your behavior pairs with those your fellow students have developed. Notice the degree of similarity of your answers.

Behavior Pairs

"Appropriate" Behavior	*"Inappropriate"* Behavior
1. _____	_____
_____	_____

"Appropriate" Behavior	"Inappropriate" Behavior
2._____	_____
_____	_____
3._____	_____
_____	_____
4._____	_____
_____	_____
5._____	_____
_____	_____

You will notice immediately that a behavior pair consists of one appropriate or desired behavior and one inappropriate or undesired behavior. Therefore, the behavior pairs represent what students should and should not do, given the teacher's classroom objectives. The behavior pairs become guidelines for classroom behavior.

Many teachers elicit the help of their students when establishing the behavior pairs. By allowing the students to have something to say about classroom guidelines and rules, these teachers have found that their students are more inclined to work within the determined behavior pairs, and the result is that the class usually runs more smoothly.

I will offer you some examples of reasonably common behavior pairs mentioned by teachers. Look at them carefully. See which ones you agree are likely to be relevant for *your* classroom. Also consider the possibility that a particular behavior pair might be appropriate for certain types of classes, while inappropriate for others. Finally, think in terms of your own philosophy of education for a moment or two while looking over the following list. Do any of the pairs "rub you the wrong way"? Do some strike you as being too strict or rigid? If so, will you disregard them completely? Or, could you modify them to a degree that would make them compatible with your philosophy and beneficial to your students? It is necessary that you consider the ramifications of your decisions regarding what will and will not be desirable behavior. Remember, your students will be influenced by what you do. Ask yourself if your influence be in their behalf.

Behavior Pairs

"Appropriate"
Behavior

"Inappropriate"
Behavior

1. Sitting in seat.	1. Walking round classroom.
2. Doing homework correctly.	2. Not doing any homework.
3. Being prepared for class.	3. Not prepared for classwork.
4. Walking in hallway.	4. Running in hallway.
5. Neat and correct work.	5. Sloppy and hurried work.
6. Attending to teacher and student discussion.	6. Talking with neighbor instead of listening.
7. Being on time to class.	7. Being late to class.
8. Becoming involved in class discussion.	8. Not participating in class discussion.
9. Showing respect.	9. Being inconsiderate of others.
10. Sharing materials.	10. Not sharing materials.
11. Raising hand before answering question.	11. Yelling out answers.
12. Being quiet while teacher or student is talking.	12. Being noisy and not listening to teacher or fellow student.
13. Exploring new materials and ideas.	13. Not trying anything new.
14. Doing class assignments.	14. Fooling around when not supposed to.
15. Doing class assignments on his own.	15. Requiring the teacher to stand over him and do the assignment for him.
16. Keeping hands to oneself.	16. Pushing and shoving.
17. Being enthusiastic.	17. Being apathetic.

For the most part, the above pairs are written as teachers gave them to me. You might find it interesting to know that number nine was by far the most frequently mentioned pair. If you will look carefully at the entire list, you will see that number nine is one of the few pairs that will require some redefining and added description. Why don't you try doing just that.

ELEVENTH YOUDOIT

What does a student have to do in order for you to know that he is being,

"Respectful"	*"Inconsiderate"*
1. _____	_____
_____	_____
2. _____	_____
_____	_____
3. _____	_____
_____	_____

PLAN AHEAD

"School is not healthy for children and other living things." Harold Sobel and Arthur E. Salz (1972) were not attempting to be humorous when they began their preface to *The Radical Papers: Readings in Education* with this quotation. Nor were they being anything but serious when they concluded the same volume with, "This book does not propose that the schools *face* a problem, it states that they *are* the problem!"

Be aware that many parents and educators are totally dissatisfied with the present state of public education. Some wish to completely abolish schools as they are today. Others wish, and are trying, to change the "system" from within. Some want something done, but they don't know what. And some just don't give a damn, one way or another. There is an awful lot of noise, constructive and destructive. In fact, Neil Postman and Charles Weingartner (1973) have entitled their newest work, *The School Book—For People Who Want To Know What All the Hollering is About.*

Up to now I have been concentrating on what you and your students will *do* in the classroom. Part of the controversy mentioned above stems from the idea that there is too much concern on the part of schools about this "doing" and not enough interest in how the child feels about what he is asked to do. There are objections to the overemphasis of academics and objections to the little time that is spent considering the child's values, self-esteem, and feelings. Dr. Terry Borton (1970) has said:

"I believe that what a student learns in school, and what he eventually becomes are significantly influenced by how he feels about himself and the world outside. I think that schools should legitimize these feelings, and should teach students a variety of ways to recognize and express them. An education without this understanding of self is simply training in an irrelevant accumulation of facts and theories—irrelevant because it is not related to what students feel is important. The goal of the teacher should be to help each student constantly increase his understanding of his feelings, and expand that self-awareness by utilizing the vast intellectual resources available to man."

I bring this controversy to your attention in the hopes that you will carefully consider and plan what *you* intend to do while in your classroom. As I see it, unless something unusual happens in the very near future, the student is going to be exposed to reading, writing, and arithmetic. He is going to be asked to look at the history of his country and world. He is going to be shown what happens when sodium and cloride are mixed; how frogs propagate; how water becomes polluted; how the sun helps plants to grow, how inventors invented; how great thinkers thought; how two apples and two more apples somehow end up being four apples. These "things" make up *part* of his academic world. But his education does not have to stop there. Again, unless things change in the very near future, students are going to have feelings, and values, and moods, and predispositions, and prejudices, and modes for relating to their fellow man. There is *no* reason why you cannot consider both of these areas while assuming the role of teacher. You *can* be concerned with student achievement *and* his feelings about himself. You *can* combine rote memory (egads!) with inquiry, problem solving, exploration, and socialization. You *can* be objective and personal at the same time. You *can* present the subject of history while discussing the importance of human values and ideals. You *can* make your classroom relevant and teach all in the same "hour." You *can* be teacher, guider, helper, and friend.

Why this "dramatic" pitch? I want you to think about your behavior pairs. Don't just arbitrarily set your pairs without considering what effect they may have on your students. If you believe that it is important for students to explore new materials, set your classroom guidelines so that exploration has a chance to take place. If you consider it important for a student to be aware of his personal values and to see how his values compare and relate to others, come up with an approach that will increase the chances that *self*-exploration will occur. Don't just scream and yell about how "bad" the educational system is. Instead, do something that will prove Charles Reich (1970) wrong when he says, in *The Greening of America:*

> "Beginning with school, if not before, an individual is systematically stripped of his imagination, his creativity, his heritage, his dreams, and his personal uniqueness. . . . Instinct, feeling, spontaneity are suppressed by overwhelming forces.

Providing
a Reason
for Doing

What a beautiful sight it is to watch a young student come bounding into a classroom, full of enthusiasm and curiosity, spontaneously exploring all that his environment has to offer. His infectious behavior spreads quickly, and, before long, all of his classmates are deeply involved in the game of learning, experiencing, and having fun.

That's a nice story, but it is all too infrequent. Some students are like our young friend, but some students aren't. Numbers are not too critical. If one isn't, you and I, as teachers, are left with an important decision. What are we going to do about the situation? My bias is straightforward. You and I have to help the "one" taste enthusiasm and curiosity. If he is not doing something that we believe would greatly enhance his opportunity for learning, then we must help him acquire whatever that something proves to be.

ONE WAY OF HELPING . . .

Suppose for a moment that a youngster enjoys receiving attention from his teacher. Suppose further that this youngster puts out considerable effort to receive his teacher's attention; that he is willing to work hard to be recognized. What do you think will happen if this youngster discovers that by doing certain things, he is attended to or recognized?

KEY:
> **Positive Reinforcer**
> *Practical definition*—Any thing, reaction, or activity that an individual is willing to put out effort to obtain; anything that he is willing to work hard for.
> *Technical definition*—Any thing, reaction, or activity that, when following a behavior, increases the likelihood that the behavior will occur more often in the future.

Billy and Miss McCawley

Miss McCawley was having difficulty with a seven-year old in her second-grade class. She described the child as very hyperactive and not at all interested in the work provided for the class. When asked what she meant by hyperactive, she indicated that the child rarely remained in his seat. For over half of the one-hour period, he would walk around the room, occasionally stopping to talk with the other pupils who were busy attending to their requested assignments.

When the child's behavior was observed, two things were noticed. First, the other children refused to talk with Billy when he came over to them. Miss McCawley had told the other children to pay no attention to Billy, and they followed her suggestion completely. Mrs. McCawley indicated that she would be the one to discipline Billy. Second, when Billy was out of his chair, his teacher would remind him that he should be sitting. She would tell him that the other children were enjoying what they were doing and he was not to bother them. She reminded him about four times each hour. Additionally, when Billy returned to his seat, the teacher would nod her head in his direction and then continue with her presentation or discussion of the day's assignment. Within a short time, Billy would once again leave his chair.

Teacher's goal: To have Billy remain in his seat when asked to do so.

TWELFTH YOUDOIT

Answer the following questions.

1. What was the desired behavior the teacher wanted?

    a. _____

2. What was the undesired behavior the teacher did not want?

    a. _____

3. Which of Billy's behaviors received the most attention from the teacher?

   a. _____

4. If Billy enjoys receiving his teacher's attention, which behavior will occur more frequently in the future?

   a. _____

5. Is the teacher going to reach her goal?

   yes   no way!

Very Important
6. Is teacher attention a positive reinforcer for Billy's behavior? How do you know? (*Hint.* Take a look at the practical definition given earlier.)

   a.   yes   no

   b. How do you know?

   _____

   _____

   _____

Miss McCawley was perplexed by her situation. She had provided Billy with various types of materials to choose from. Even when he would make a selection, he would still end up wandering around the room.

It was suggested to the teacher that she might, quite by accident, be maintaining Billy's wandering. It was pointed out that possibly her verbal attention, telling Billy to sit down, which was given *when* the youngster was out of his chair, might be more important to him (a stronger reinforcer) than the nod given *when* Billy was in his chair. Finally, it was suggested that if Miss McCawley wanted Billy to sit, then perhaps she should provide a reason for him to be in his chair. Instead of saying nothing when he was seated, why not praise him a little for the more desired behavior?

Miss McCawley no longer reminded Billy to sit down. Instead, when he was in his chair working, she would occasionally walk over to him and while touching his shoulder, tell him how much she appreciated his sitting and working. She would withhold her attention when he was doing something else other than what was considered appropriate and give him a lot of attention and praise when he was behaving as she wished.

By the end of the week, Billy was sitting in his chair and working for about the same amount of time as the other children in the class.

Question. What was the major thing Miss McCawley did in order to change Billy's wandering behavior?

a. _____

_____

I am going to present a composite "before" and "after" picture of Billy's behavior, the teacher's reactions, and the resulting effects of Miss McCawley's actions. Please look at it carefully. Before long, I will ask you to fill in the blanks, and I would like you to be familiar with the format.

Teacher's Initial Program		
Behavior	Environment's Reaction	Results
Desired (Sitting in chair)	Teacher's reaction— Nod; little if any reinforcement	*Decrease* in Billy's sitting
Undesired (Out of chair)	Teacher's reaction— telling Billy to sit down; attention and recognition	*Increase* in Billy being out of chair

Teacher's New Program		
Behavior	Environment's Reaction	Results
Desired (Sitting in chair)	Teacher's reaction— A good deal of praise and attention	*Increase* in Billy's sitting
Undesired (Out of chair)	Teacher's reaction— No attention whatsoever	*Decrease* in Billy being out of chair

KEY:

> Whatever the behavior that occurs immediately prior to the teacher's reinforcement is the behavior most likely to increase in the future.

"CAUSE"

Before we look at the implications of the above key, let me ask you a question. Are you at all curious as to why Billy was walking around the classroom in the first place? What event(s) might have been responsible for his behavior?

THIRTEENTH YOUDOIT

Spend a few minutes in class discussing possible "causes" for Billy's behavior. Once you have made several suggestions, see if you can determine whether any of the suggestions is the "real reason" why Billy was walking. The following are some ideas you might consider.

1. He is upset.
2. He has to take a test.
3. His teacher's reactions to his walking.
4. He was born under the sign of Gemini.

What you probably found was that determining and verifying the "real reason" why a youngster does something is more difficult than it first seems. This is particularly the case if you indicate that something is wrong with the youngster (e.g., the first of the four ideas presented above). More times than not, that is exactly what happens. We find ourselves saying that the student is "upset," or that he is "anxious and nervous." Understand, he may well be upset or nervous, it is just difficult for us to know this. We can ask him, of course, but even he might not be able to tell us. In place of asking, we often assume that something is wrong, and our assumption is based on what we observe him doing. For example, when we see someone crying we are inclined to assume that he is unhappy. The problem with this is that not everyone cries when they are unhappy, and a lot of us cry when we are not at all unhappy. Crying, then, is rarely enough for us to be certain that the individual is unhappy. In the same vein, walking around a room, biting fingernails, or tapping a pencil on a desk are insufficient bits of information on which to base a statement about what is wrong or why a youngster is doing something. Yet, if you were inclined to agree with the first of the four ideas I offered you, you used Billy's walking as an indication of his being upset, and then you said that he is walking because he is upset. If you look carefully at that sequence, I think you will see that it doesn't make much sense. (Why is he walking? Because he is upset. How do you know he is upset? Because he is walking.) By the way, if Billy stops walking, does that mean that he is no longer upset?

If you preferred my second or third idea, then you have partially avoided saying something is wrong with Billy. Those two ideas focus more directly on his environment. At the same time, neither idea tells us "why" he walks. Instead, the two ideas suggest *conditions* under which Billy is likely to walk. Let me show you what I mean. Suppose that we have observed Billy wandering each time a test is about to be given. Should we say that he walks around because of the test? (We probably want to say that he walks because he is "nervous," but that would bring us back to the nonsensical sequence.) Let's see what happens if the teacher calls off the test. Billy sits! Then she changes her mind once again. Up goes Billy. Is that enough evidence to say that he walks *because* of the test? Nope! He might be walking "because" he has learned that if he walks enough, he gets sent from the room and thus avoids the test. That is a possibility. Or he might have discovered that by walking immediately before a test he feels more comfortable and does better on the test, and that is why he walks. Or he might have learned that if he walks enough, the teacher will take the test for him. (There are probably ten other "or's.") Is Billy's "up" and "down" behavior enough evidence to say something? Yes. We can say that given the condition of a test, Billy is likely to walk around. And that is about all we can say for sure.

We can't say much more than that even when the teacher changes her reactions to Billy's behavior and his behavior changes. Granted, when Miss McCawley attended to Billy when he walked, his walking increased. When she changed, and praised his sitting, that behavior began to occur more often. But that still is not enough evidence to be absolutely certain that her reactions were the "real reasons" for his behavior. Again, all we can justifiably say is that given the condition of praise for sitting, sitting is more likely to occur. Given the condition of attention for walking, walking will occur more often.

The point of this discussion is that determining the "causes" and "why's" of behavior is extremely difficult. Educators and psychologists today rarely speak in terms of "cause" and "effect." Instead, they speak of conditions and behaviors occurring together. Given the condition, the behavior is likely to happen. Given the absence of the condition, the behavior is less likely to happen. In most cases, we do not even know why the conditions and behavior go together; they just seem to more times than not. Be cautious, therefore, when you are asked to explain why a particular behavior occurs. Your incorrect answer may do extensive harm to the youngster. (Check some elementary school records and I think you will see what I mean.) Even a correct answer, unless it can be worked with, will serve little purpose. Do not be ashamed to admit that you do not know why a student is doing something. Be more concerned with the conditions under which the behavior is occurring and what you, as the teacher, are doing under those conditions. If your reactions and his behavior are occurring jointly and, if what he is doing is viewed as inappropriate, you are going to have to work with your "doing" before you can expect the student to change. That will be much more helpful to the student than any philosophizing as to the "why's."

ONE WAY OF HELPING. . . .INCENTIVES

Try It, You'll Like It

Mr. Haber had developed what he thought was a very exciting program for his third-grade science class. The topic dealt with water pollution and how it was spreading all over the world. For some reason, his class did not share his enthusiasm. Perhaps, because it was early spring, the children's fancies had turned to something else. Be that as it may, he was determined to introduce this topic to them, hoping eventually they would not only become interested, but would come to realize its seriousness.

He had set up a series of "stations" in his classroom. Each station brought up one point, through demonstration or reading material, and set the stage for the introduction to a further point to be covered at a following station.

Despite his efforts, few of the students became involved in the project. He decided, therefore, to try something. On the following day, he asked the children to take their seats. "If you had your choice," he asked, "what would you like to do today?" A few of the students said they wanted to go home and go swimming. But the majority of them indicated that they would love to go outside and play in the sunshine.

He, too, was tempted by that idea. "Okay, I'll tell you what we will do. Our class period is for forty-five minutes. We will all work real hard on our ecology project for thirty-five minutes, then we'll go outside and run around together. Is that fair?" The children's response was as he hoped. There was unanimous agreement that his idea was not only fair, but great.

The children accomplished more in the thirty-five minutes than they had during the previous three days. He kept the agreement going for the next two weeks (the duration of the ecology project). Some of the children decided that instead of going outside, which they would be able to do as soon as the school day ended, they preferred to stay in the class and talk about the project.

Mr. Haber felt so positive about the outcome of his idea that he incorporated it into several other projects and assignments. On some occasions, instead of going outside, the children were given the option to sit in the back of the classroom and look at magazines he had brought, or quietly talk with one another, or go to the school's learning center to watch film strips about the Grand Canyon, the Rocky Mountains, or whatever. From the students' viewpoint, the classroom was a super place to be.

Obviously, Mr. Haber provided what he would call an incentive for his students. He offered them something that would please them; something they could have as soon as they completed what was agreed to be a reasonable amount of work. He believed it was important to help start the "interested" behavior going. For him, a brief free-time period was a way for him to accomplish his goal, and it was one way for him to help his students become involved in a topical issue.

"THAT REALLY BOTHERS ME"

"I can't disagree or find much fault with your last two examples," Miss Martin began. "I'm certain all of us are guilty, sometime or another, of what your Miss McCawley did. And I guess there are some teachers who would agree with Mr. Haber's approach. But, at the same time, what you are saying really bothers me. First, I'd like to know what Miss McCawley did with the other twenty-nine students while she spent all her time reinforcing Billy when he sat down. Did she just ignore the rest of the children?"

"Besides that," she continued without waiting for an answer from the speaker, "I know you are going to tell us that we must begin to reward our students for good behavior and I, personally, can't accept that for several reasons. First, it is a form of bribery. That is disturbing to me and to everyone else here. Second, by starting the reinforcement stuff you are creating a situation where a child is going to come to expect a reward for everything he does—and that's not realistic. Third, our students should do certain things because it is the right thing to do. They shouldn't do it for an award. . .I mean, reward. That's like asking a child to read a book, not for the sake of the knowledge in the book, but for a piece of candy or something like that—like what Mr. Haber did. That really bothers me!"

As quickly as Miss Martin sat down, another teacher, in the back of the auditorium, waved her outstretched hand as if wanting to be recognized. The speaker looked in her direction and with a broad smile asked, "Friend or foe?"

Returning the smile, the teacher said, "I think I am going to be a friend."

"Thanks," the speaker immediately responded, "but let me have about two seconds and then the floor is yours."

Looking toward Miss Martin, the speaker began. "I am glad that you have brought up these issues. They are very important to most of us. I'll try to answer some of your arguments but, for now, my 'friend' has the floor." The speaker motioned to the teacher in the back of the room. As she stood, he sat down in a chair next to the podium.

"I've given a lot of thought," the teacher began, "to some of the things Kathy (Miss Martin) just mentioned, probably because I, too, was concerned—particularly about the bribery business and doing certain things just because it's the right thing to do."

"As I see it," she continued, "when we hear the word bribery, we usually hear it in context with one of our political officials where they have taken money or gifts for some illegal activity. I think all of us agree that's bad. But when I think of using reinforcers in my classroom I see the situation as being totally different. First, the behaviors that we work with in class are, hopefully, far from illegal—like helping a youngster read a little better or learn a new concept. By the way, Kathy, you and I are reinforced for our behavior—we do receive a paycheck every once in a while, and I doubt that we consider our teaching to be illegal."

"Our paychecks are too small to be considered bribes," added another teacher, which resulted in resounding laughter and applause from the audience.

"Come on, Jack, I'm being serious," the first teacher commented.

"So am I," Jack said, resulting in more laughter. "Okay, I'm sorry, Anne. I know you are being serious."

"Besides," Anne continued, "we use reinforcers all the time in our rooms without even realizing it, even you, Kathy. We praise children for their good efforts; we do not hesitate to give them A's and write words of appreciation on their papers when they have done an excellent job. That's not bribery, is it? Sometimes we allow our students to be first in the lunch line when they have done well; we smile and pat them on the back when they've tried something never attempted before; I know, Kathy, that every once in a while *you* give your kids a few extra minutes of free time when their work has been outstanding. Those are all potential reinforcers. We don't consider them forms of bribery, do we?"

"Reinforcers are signs of appreciation and recognition—in the same way that an Oscar award is given to an actress for a fine performance, or a merit badge is given to a cub scout, or the Congressional Medal of Honor is given for recognition of bravery."

"Kathy, let me ask you a question," Anne said turning toward Miss Martin. "Suppose that you spent four hours baking your handsome husband a chocolate cake and after eating some of it, he never said a word to you. How would you react?"

"That would be the last chocolate cake he ever saw," Kathy laughingly answered.

"What would you have wanted him to do?"

"A small sign of appreciation wouldn't have hurt," Kathy answered.

"Think about that for a moment," Anne responded, giving Miss Martin a few seconds to think about what she had just said.

"I see what you are saying, and I guess it does make some sense," Miss Martin began, "but I still think children should do things because. . .well. . .just because they should."

"Kathy, many children do just that or, at least, it seems that way to us. You have John Hess in your reading class, don't you?"

"Yes, I do."

"Do you have to reinforce him for reading a book?"

"Never."

"John Hess, if my memory serves me correctly, loves to read. Reading is 'intrinsically' reinforcing to John. He seems to get a great deal of pleasure from reading. But how about some of the others in your class? Not all of them have found reading to be so enjoyable. So maybe what you and I do is to use a little reinforcement, some praise or a few minutes of extra recess, to get the reading behavior going in the hopes that it will become intrinsically reinforcing. That's the name of the game for me. If a child doesn't do something that is, perhaps, best for him in the long run, what good does it do to simply say, you should do it because you should; or you should do it because you are in fifth grade; or you should do it because you are old enough to be able to do it? Those 'shoulds' just don't make any sense. They don't help the child much, either. While you and I sit and argue the merits, or lack of merits, for the occassional use of reinforcement, some of our students get further and further behind. While we enjoy waving our theoretical flags, our students' chances for success and confidence diminsh."

"Some students," Anne continued, "appear to require very little reinforcement from us, John Hess, for example. But have you met John's parents? If you have, you know that his parents are very appreciative of his efforts, and they *demonstrate* their appreciation to John. John has learned that his parents are pleased with his work and he apparently enjoys pleasing them. He talks with his parents about what he has read, and that is highly reinforcing in itself." Then, turning toward Miss Martin, Anne asked, "Kathy, have you met Billy James' parents?"

"No, I haven't."

"Well, as a matter of fact, I haven't, either. They have never come to a parent-teacher meeting. They have never answered any of the notes I have sent to them. In fact, Billy has confided in me that his parents really don't care much, so why should he. My feeling is that we, his teachers, have to provide him with a reason to start learning, to become interested in something. If we don't, who will?"

"I never thought about it," Miss Martin answered.

"Well, my dear, we'd better start thinking about it. You know, if we fail to provide him with something positive to work *for,* we are going to end up providing him with something 'unpleasant' to work to *avoid,* such as our punishment."

"I'm not certain that I understand that," Miss Martin said.

"You will in just a while," Anne responded.

PROVIDING YOUR STUDENTS WITH SOMETHING TO WORK FOR

Unless you find yourself teaching in a closet, with no students, you are going to find yourself using some positive reinforcement in your classroom. Every teacher does. Even the most vociferous critic "breaks down" and uses it, even if it is "only" a pat on the back, a smile, a word of praise, or a "thank you."

The fact of saying that you will use positive reinforcement, however, is not the same as saying that you will use it correctly. For example:

1. Accidentally, you may end up increasing or maintaining a behavior that was unintended (remember Miss McCawley).
2. There will be times, of course, when you will offer it to your students. But because of what you have asked them to do, there is no way they will ever receive it.
3. There will be times you give it, when you shouldn't.
4. There will be times you do not give it, when you should.

Confusing you a little more,

5. There will be times you think you *are* using it, when you will not be.
6. There will be times you are certain that you are *not* using it, when, in fact, you will be.

Despite what you may have read or heard, effective use of positive reinforcement is just a little more difficult than "popping" M & M's.

Do You Have a Reinforcer?

Experienced teachers know that certain activities or responses are reinforcing to some students and not reinforcing to others. They will tell you that it is rare to find one reinforcer that will "turn on" an entire class. They will tell you that some students find reading highly reinforcing, while others do not. Some students work like beavers to collect gold stars, others turn their noses up at the idea. Some students work very hard for words of praise, while some work very hard just to be left alone.

KEY: | Whether an event, activity, or reaction is a positive reinforcer can only be known after seeing what effect the reaction has on a student's behavior. If the event is applied immediately after the behavior and that behavior begins to occur more often in the future, then whatever has been applied is called a positive reinforcer.

Imagine the parent who says to her young son, "Honey, as soon as you finish your homework, Mother is going to give you a big bowl of spinach!" If spinach is not one of the child's priority vegetables, I think you can guess the child's remarks. On the other hand, if Popeye is one of the child's heros, the homework may be completed in record time.

One of the first points you must keep in mind is that before you can use positive reinforcement to help a student learn something, you must first have a positive reinforcer. You must have something the student is willing to work for. If you provide something that you believe is a reinforcer, but for the student it is not, he is not likely to put out much effort to obtain it. Remember, the student's behavior, not your belief, is the best barometer to determine whether you have a reinforcer. (Go back, for a moment, to the ninth youdoit, p. 38. Were your ideas correct or, having read this last key, would you change what you said?)

"Must I Reinforce Every Child?"

My first answer is "No, you don't have to." My second answer, which is more accurate, is that it depends on the student. Some students will do just fine on their own. A few smiles or words of praise will be more than enough to maintain their appropriate behavior for long periods of time. Some students won't even need that. Their parents reinforce their efforts. Some students will have already found the work to be intrinsically enjoyable; doing the work in itself is reinforcing enough. But some students *will* need your help. They will need your encouragement and incentives. You will need to provide them with a reason for doing.

TYPES OF POSITIVE REINFORCEMENT APPROACHES

We will now look at various reinforcement approaches. Some are extremely simple, while others are very complex. They do not have to be used precisely as I will describe them; they can be varied to fit the style of classroom (e.g., "open" or "self-contained") in which you will teach. They also can be modified to fit your classroom objectives. I think you will find it helpful if, while reading about the different approaches, you talk with teachers who are using them, or have used them, to see the types of problems, if any, they have experienced.

SOCIAL REINFORCEMENT

Fortunately, for our students, the easiest type of reinforcement we can use also happens to be the most important type. So important is it that it *must* be used along with all the other approaches. Praise, attention, recognition, smiles, pats on the back, compliments, words of thanks, are examples of social reinforcers. They can be used to help us increase a wide variety of behaviors. They also help students feel good about themselves. Without them, classrooms would not only be sad, but unbearable.

Almost every student is willing to work hard to obtain attention. Attention and affection, then, are powerful aides for teaching. And what is so nice about attention and affection is that they are with us all the time. We do not have to go to the store or learning center to pick them up.

Not Quite a Wilt Chamberlain

Mr. Dobbs decided the time had come to help one of his second-grade physical education students. Jamie was the smallest boy in the class, and he was having a terrible time getting a basketball to come anywhere near the basket. When the class first began "playing" basketball, Jamie tried as hard as anyone. But it seemed as the days passed his efforts became more infrequent. When the time came for Jamie to have his turn, the flight of his ball resembled that of an old and very tired duck. Dejectedly, Jamie would turn around and walk to the end of the line.

Mr. Dobbs could tell that Jamie certainly had the strength to put the ball close to the basket, but he believed that since Jamie had met with such little success, he simply wasn't interested in trying anymore.

When Jamie returned to the front of the line, Mr. Dobbs walked up right next to him. "Give it a good shot," Mr. Dobbs said quietly. Jamie looked up toward his coach, smiled, and let the ball fly. As luck would have it, the ball just about reached the backboard—which was quite good compared with what happened the last time. "Hey, not bad. That was pretty close," Mr. Dobbs said as he patted Jamie's shoulder. With a broadened smile, Jamie quickly retrieved the ball, gave it to the next boy in line, and ran to the back of the line. Not wanting to make Jamie think that he was being singled out, Mr. Dobbs made it a point to compliment some of the other boys for their efforts. When Jamie returned to the front, he was quickly joined by Mr. Dobbs. "Try to aim for that backboard, okay?"

"Okay," Jamie responded.

Jamie spent several seconds stabilizing his stance, placing his hands on the ball just as he wanted, and looking up toward the backboard. Just before he threw the ball he gave a quick glance toward Mr. Dobbs. "Looks good," Mr. Dobbs said. Up went the ball and smack into the left side of the backboard. "Super—you hit it! Pretty soon you will throw it right in the basket." The truth is that it took several days before Mr. Dobbs was able to bellow, "Two points!"

What was important to Mr. Dobbs, at least, was the fact that Jamie was trying as hard as he was during the first days of the basketball class.

If you have ever taken a shot at a new sport and failed to set the world on fire right off the bat, you know how Jamie was feeling. It is not much fun to put out a lot of effort and get very little, if anything, in return. All Mr. Dobbs did was to help Jamie start trying again. As soon as Jamie made a couple of baskets on his own, he began to get a good deal of recognition from his friends. When one of his classmates came over to him and gave him "five fingers," Mr. Dobbs knew that if Jamie could grow about six feet taller he could probably play for the Lakers.

Correct Answers Aren't Everything

Mary Jo rarely said anything in her American History class. She appeared attentive to class discussions but, when the time came for the students to volunteer answers to presented questions, Mary Jo tried to make herself invisible.

One of the objectives the teacher set for the class was lively student interaction. On occasion, she would ask for volunteers to debate issues that were controversial in the early days of American independence. Most of the students seem to enjoy the debating, but Mary Jo never volunteered. On a recent test, the teacher posed a question to her class about one of the debated issues, and Mary Jo's written answer was very good. The teacher decided to ask Mary Jo to stay after class so she could talk to her about the answer.

"The answer on your test was really very good. In fact, it was one of the best I have ever received."

"Thank you," Mary Jo responded. "I took my time and thought about the answer before I wrote anything."

"I just wanted you to know that I was very pleased," the teacher said.

On the following day in class, the teacher decided to discuss some of the papers submitted by the students. One of the first papers discussed was Mary Jo's. After mentioning some of the points Mary Jo had described so accurately, the teacher turned toward her and asked her a question about one of the factual aspects of her answer. The teacher suddenly realized that for the first time, she had put Mary Jo on the spot. She was quite upset with herself for doing so. Although Mary Jo hesitated for a brief moment, she offered an answer to her teacher's question. Unfortunately, she missed the date of the Boston Tea Party by ten years. Although the teacher knew that the answer was incorrect, she also knew that she had been presented with a golden opportunity to praise Mary Jo's effort. This was just about the first time Mary Jo had said anything in front of the class. "That's just about right, Mary Jo, thank you. Actually, the Tea Party was in 1773, but the date isn't that critical. What is much more important was your very accurate analysis of what led up to the incident. Again, Mary Jo, very good."

Do you agree with the teacher's approach? Imagine, for a moment, what would have happened to Mary Jo's *future* efforts had the teacher simply responded that her answer regarding the date was wrong and dropped the matter right there. Instead, the teacher wisely decided to praise Mary Jo's efforts, hoping that the social reinforcement would help Mary Jo feel comfortable enough to try volunteering an answer in the near future.

Using Social Reinforcement Effectively

Social reinforcement will be extremely effective if you will keep three ideas in mind: the idea of immediacy, the idea of potency, and the idea of description.

Immediacy

The closer the social reinforcer is to the behavior, the greater the chances the reinforced behavior will increase. You will want to keep the time period between the behavior and your response as short as possible. This is particularly the case with young students. As soon as you see a behavior that you consider desirable, a word of praise or thanks, a little recognition, or pat on the back will increase your chances of seeing that behavior again. For the older students, a certain amount of delay is tolerable but, again, try to keep your delay to a minimum. Even adults have a hard time accepting delays. A phone call thanking a host and hostess for a lovely evening, three weeks after a dinner party, may not do the trick.

Potency

There is, of course, no guarantee that our words of praise and recognition will be reinforcing. Social reinforcers obtain and maintain their potency because they are occasionally associated with other types of reinforcers. In a school setting, these reinforcers can be consumable types, such as milk, cookies, or a piece of candy. However, they do not have to be. Anything that is extremely reinforcing to a student can help to maintain the effectiveness of social reinforcers. For example, extra recess, free-time periods, and special trips to zoos and museums can serve the same purpose. You really do not have to worry too much about this potency issue, because the associating effect between social reinforcers and the other types of reinforcers works automatically. Each time you associate yourself and your words of praise with the extra recess, an exciting class project, or a special trip, you are helping to maintain the reinforcing quality of your "thanks" and signs of appreciation.

Description

Whenever possible, try to describe specifically the exact behavior that warranted your recognition and praise. "Thank you, Johnny for raising your hand," will not only help maintain Johnny's efforts, but will also tell him which behavior pleased you. If Mary is sitting, quietly writing her assignment, and you walk by and say, "Very good," she may think you are reinforcing her for tapping her foot on the floor (which you didn't see). If, instead, you were particularly pleased with her writing efforts, then a statement to that effect will be much more meaningful to both of you.

How about Sincerity?

There will be times when you won't feel like praising or thanking a youngster when he finally does something that was desired. This is often the case when the student has been misbehaving for many minutes. As hard as it may be for you, you must make every effort to "catch him when he is doing something good." Although we have not discussed this, I think you may have guessed that if an infrequent behavior finally occurs and it is not followed by some form of reinforcement, the chances are the behavior will not occur again for some time. If we allow our negative mood to prevent us from calling attention to the desired behavior, we hurt ourselves as well as the student. He is less likely to repeat the appropriate behavior and, perhaps, more likely to continue his misbehavior, which will heighten our negative mood. That is not a very desirable cycle. "But if I don't really mean it, won't he be able to tell?" *Yes*, if you allow your "don't really mean it" attitude to shine through. A gruff "Thanks" will come across much differently than a pleasant, animated "Thanks." Something less than sage advice, don't be gruff! It may appear noble to say to yourself, "Well, he finally did something helpful, but since I honestly do not feel like thanking him, I won't." Noble, perhaps, but a solution to your problems? No way! Think how sincerely appreciative you will feel when he begins to behave more appropriately. Help him (and yourself) a little. When he does behave appropriately, demonstrate your appreciation. Otherwise your day may be long and totally downhill, and so may the student's.

Social Reinforcement Can Work Against You

Just about every teacher, including myself, has at one time or another socially reinforced a behavior, without meaning to increase it. If we do not watch which behaviors we are attending to, some of them may end up on the undesirable side of our behavior pairs.

Tapping the Time Away

Henry and Peter had been friends for a long time. When they discovered they had both been assigned to fourth-period Spanish, they were thrilled—not thrilled with Spanish, but thrilled with the idea that they would be able to horse around together. It didn't take Mr. Arens long to find out that the two boys could find many ways to avoid doing their work. Since they sat next to one another, it was easy for them to distract each other. They would pass notes, talk behind cupped hands, and become hysterical practicing the "rolling" letter "r"; on occasion they would have thumb fights, and they carried on a never-ending game of "dots."

Mr. Arens had first asked them and later told them to behave themselves, but his warnings seemed to have little effect on reducing their shenanigans. Finally, he decided to separate them. The boys were not pleased with the new seating arrangement but, being the troupers they were, their games were only temporarily delayed.

Bored with what was going on in the class, Peter began, rather innocently, to tap his pencil on his desk. The sound went unnoticed by just about everyone except Henry, who was busy thinking about what he could do besides the classwork. Without hesitation, Henry began echoing his friend's tapping, and a new game was born. Peter would tap twice, and Henry would quickly do the same. Before long they were practicing their own version of Morse Code.

"All right, now both of you stop that this minute," Mr. Arens warned. "I will not tell you again."

Unfortunately, he did not keep his word. Before the Spanish class was over, he had given them three more warnings. As soon as the warnings came, the boys would drop their pencils and pick up their Spanish books. They must, however, have been looking through them instead of at them, because as soon as Mr. Arens turned his back, the "messages"once again began.

"How many more times must I tell you to stop?" the teacher questioned.

Although no answer was offered, twenty-five would have been accurate. The more often he told them, the more often the class was interrupted by the syncopated sounds of the not too distant drummers.

In many cases, the behaviors that create minor problems in our classrooms are the very behaviors that receive most of our attention. Equally as important, we often fail to call attention to a more desired alternative behavior. In Mr. Arens' case, his warnings and yelling were forms of attention, given immediately after the boys' mischievous behavior. Since their behavior increased and then was maintained at a fairly frequent level, the teacher's "negative" attention was, in fact, a social reinforcer for the boys.

Getting More for Being Away

Miss Rhodes would have her kindergarten children sit in a semicircle when it came time to practice numbers and letters. She would go around the semicircle asking each youngster in turn to repeat a sound or a number. Many minutes would pass by before she would go from one end of the class to the other. The children would fidget in their seats and talk to one another while waiting for their turn.

Dotty was one of the more quiet children in the group. She sat at the very end of the semicircle. There would be times when Dotty would be attended to very infrequently. For example, if one of the other children was having difficulty with a particular sound, the teacher would spend considerable time with that child without involving the others.

During one class, Dotty moved her chair slightly away from the semicircle. With each passing minute she moved further and further away. Pretty soon, she was physically out of the group. "Won't you come back and join us?" Miss Rhodes asked politely. Quickly, Dotty moved her chair back. Miss Rhodes thanked Dotty and then continued with her lesson. Within a few minutes, Dotty once again departed. Again, she was asked to come back, and again she did. This time, however, nothing else was said.

By the end of the week, Dotty was away from the group more times then she was in it. On one occasion, the teacher stopped what she was doing and pulled her chair alongside Dotty's—which was now well away from her classmates. The teacher spent several minutes alone with Dotty asking her to come back, telling her how much "fun" it was for everyone to work together, and mentioning that her friends would miss her if she sat so far away.

These "conversations" began to occur more frequently, and Dotty had little difficulty finding out that the longer she stayed away, the more her teacher would talk with her.

Once again, without realizing it, the teacher began paying much more attention to the very behavior she believed inappropriate. She failed to realize that her social reinforcement just as easily would increase and maintain the "away" behavior as it would increase and maintain being with the group.

Let's look at a youdoit. See what you would do if you were Miss Rhodes.

FOURTEENTH YOUDOIT

I am going to present you with a "before" and "after" chart. I will supply you with the behaviors in question, and I would like you to fill in the remaining blocks. In this situation, the "before" represents what Miss Rhodes is *now* doing and the effect she is having. The "after" should represent what you think she *should* do.

Teacher's Initial Program ("Before")		
Behavior	Environment's Reaction	Results
Desired (Being with group)	Teacher's reaction—	
Undesired (Being away from group)	Teacher's reaction—	

Teacher's New Program ("After")		
Behavior	Environment's Reaction	
Desired (Being with group)	Teacher's reaction—	
Undesired (Being away from group)	Teacher's reaction—	

I have provided a possible answer to the above chart. Our answers, of course, will not be the same. But as long as you realize that the critical issue deals with the question of *which* of the student's behaviors receives the majority of the teacher's social reinforcement, and you effectively deal with that problem, then you have the point. (You might take a moment or two during class to compare your answer with those of your classmates.)

Initial Program		
Behavior	Environment's Reaction	Results
Desired (Being with group)	Teacher's reaction— Little, if any social reinforcement	*decrease* in being with group
Undesired (Being away from group)	Teacher's reaction – Coaxing to come back; considerable attention	*increase* in being away from group

New Program	
Behavior	Environment's Reaction
Desired (Being with group)	Teacher's reaction— Demonstrated attention and appreciation; considerable social reinforcement
Undesired (Being away from group)	Teacher's reaction— *One* pleasant request that Dotty return; thereafter, no coaxing, no social reinforcement

Notice that I suggested that the teacher give Dotty one request to return to the group. Based on the information that I offered in the scenario, there is a good chance that Dotty will comply with the teacher's request. If she does, then the teacher has the opportunity to use her social reinforcement for her goal right away. However, if Dotty does not return immediately, the teacher should avoid additional requests, at least for that day. The reason for avoiding continued requesting is that it is a form of coaxing, and possible reinforcement, and it will ultimately work against the teacher.

What should the teacher do if Dotty simply does not come back when asked? There are several things the teacher can consider. First, providing a group activity with special interest for Dotty would probably solve the problem. If the teacher knows of something Dotty is interested in, and she includes that topic or activity into the group situation, Dotty will probably return. If so, social reinforcement is very important. The teacher should also consider using her social reinforcement for any of Dotty's slight moves toward the group. This point deals with the reinforcing of gradual improvement, and we will refer back to it several times. For example, the chair being moved in the direction of the group, or Dotty looking toward the group, or Dotty commenting on what the group is doing, is all the teacher will need to help Dotty become involved. As soon as the teacher observes any of these slight moves (or others, equally as appropriate), she should immediately call attention to Dotty's efforts. She should *not* wait until Dotty is in the group before demonstrating her appreciation. Instead, she should praise Dotty's *gradual improvement* and effort.

Getting More for Doing Less

One of Mrs. Page's most important classroom goals was to have her students learn to work on their own. For her, independent work by a student meant that the student was mature and responsible. Her class format was set up to increase the chances that her students would attend to their tasks without requiring much assistance from her. For the most part, she was very successful. She provided work sheets that covered the day's assignments. Each student was familiarized with what was expected of him. Any questions the students had regarding the material were answered carefully. When everyone appeared to know what they were to do, the independent work period began. As the students were working, Mrs. Page would walk around the class, commenting to each student about their work. Usually, the teacher's comments dealt with how nicely the students were doing on their own.

She was, however, having a problem with one of the boys. According to Mrs. Page, Dicky seemed to require more attention than any of the other students. During just about every independent work period, Dicky would raise his hand, requesting help from Mrs. Page. She would go to him when his hand was raised and, before she would help him, she would tell him that he must learn to work on his own like the rest of the students. He would usually agree with her but, after being left alone for several minutes, his hand would once again be raised, and Mrs. Page would assist him.

On one particular day, when Dicky had received assistance five times, the teacher told Dicky that she was not coming over until he began to work on his own. The teacher's ultimatum was apparently effective, since Dicky worked several minutes without raising his hand. The teacher noticed him working but decided to require that he spend a little more time on his task before she would walk over to him to check his work. The next time she looked in his direction she saw that he had stopped working completely; his pencil was by his paper, and he was looking around the room. She immediately went over to him and asked, "Why have you stopped? Are you finished?"

Dicky said to her, "I haven't finished, but I can't do this problem."

"Now Dicky, you finished the same problem yesterday. I know you can do it."

"Well, I just don't think I can," Dicky answered.

"All right," Mrs. Page said, "I will help you this one more time, but then you will have to complete the assignment by yourself."

"Okay," Dicky agreed.

Dicky, however, did not complete his assignment. Instead, he requested and received Mrs. Page's assistance several times that day and many days thereafter.

In a conversation with Mrs. Page, I was told that Dicky was doing less work; that he was requesting more help; and he was "daydreaming" more often. She *concluded* that Dicky was too immature to handle the independent work; she, therefore, decided to spend more time helping him with his assignments.

FIFTEENTH YOUDOIT

I want you to fill in the following chart. When you have completed the chart, please reread the last paragraph in the above scenerio. Is there anything about the teacher's conclusion that bothers you? The point that I am after is quite subtle. See if you can find it. If you can't, you will find it on p. 71.

Teacher's Initial Program		
Behavior	Environment's Reaction	Results
Desired (Independent work)	Teacher's reaction—	
Undesired (Requiring much assistance)	Teacher's reaction—	

Teacher's New Program	
Behavior	Environment's Reaction
Desired (Independent work)	Teacher's reaction—
Undesired (Requiring much assistance)	Teacher's reaction—

Do you remember the introduced point about gradual improvement? In my view, Mrs. Page goofed. She had the perfect opportunity to help Dicky, but she let it go by. Do you agree that Dicky did demonstrate the desired behavior?

Responsibility—Do Not Place It "Inside" the Student Too Quickly

Mrs. Page concluded that Dicky was too "immature" to handle independent work. She very nicely and safely determined that something was wrong with Dicky. She placed the responsibility for the "absence" of the desired behavior *inside* him—*HE* is too immature! That, hopefully, bothered you. In the first place, Dicky *did* demonstrate the desired behavior,

> The teacher noticed him working (for several minutes) but decided to require that he spend a little more time on his task before she would walk over to him to check his work. (From ms. p. 69)

She could have helped herself and Dicky had she praised his efforts while he was working. He had tried, so why not call attention to his trying?

In the second place, had she looked at her *own* behavior and asked the question about what effect she might be having on Dicky's behavior, she might not have jumped to her erroneous conclusion. How about these questions?

QUESTION. How do you know that Dicky is too immature?
ANSWER. Well, he is not working independently.
QUESTION. Does that mean that if he were to start working independently that he would not be immature, or at least not as immature?
ANSWER. I guess so.
QUESTION. Then why not praise him when he begins to work by himself, even if he only works independently for a few minutes? That is a beginning!
ANSWER. I guess so.
RESPONSE. Right!

SIXTEENTH YOUDOIT

Remember Dotty and her moving away from the group? How would you react if you were told, by her teacher, that Dotty continued to move her chair away because she had a "short attention span?" (Don't just say, "Hogwash!")

Your reaction

1. _____

_____

_____

_____

_____

_____

2. *Hogwash!*

Summary and Usefulness

Walk into any classroom and watch a teacher who uses a good deal of social reinforcement and you will see a beautiful thing: the teacher and students enjoy being with one another. Walk into a classroom where there is little, if any, praise, recognition, and warmth, and you will probably feel drained very shortly. Imagine how the students feel.

Social reinforcement will effectively increase many behaviors, some desirable, some not so desirable. What you intend to increase may not be what you do increase. It is very important, therefore, that you carefully watch the behaviors receiving your attention. In most cases, the behavior that occurs immediately prior to your attention will be the behavior that is affected. Think about the behaviors and activities that you believe are appropriate for your classroom and for your students. When you observe the behaviors, make an effort to call attention to them. Your students will appreciate it.

Social reinforcement is most effective with people who are somewhere between 4 and 44,444 days old. It, therefore, has its limits. Fortunately, however, all your students' ages will fall somewhere in between the limitations.

GRANDMA'S RULE AND PREMACK PRINCIPLE

There will be times when you will find it very helpful to consider a second reinforcement approach along with your social reinforcement.

One of the main advantages of this second approach is that the student's own behavior, or voiced desire, literally lets you know what he presently values.

KEY:	Any activity or behavior a student does very often, or any activity he desires to experience, can be used as a reinforcer for some activity you would like him to do.

Grandma's rule is an appropriate name for this procedure because grandmas (and mothers, fathers, and teachers) have been using it for a lot longer than you and I (and our mothers and fathers and teachers) have been around. The rule simply states that a student can have access to what he would like *after* he has completed what you would like him to do. "You may have recess period as soon as you correctly finish your math problems," is an example of Grandma's rule, assuming you know that the student enjoys recess. If your mother ever told you that you could have your apple pie as soon as you finished your dinner, then you have experienced Grandma's rule. Notice that the rule, when used correctly, is *always* stated in the positive. Notice also that both the desired behavior and the reinforcer are made very clear to the student. "If you do not clean your desk area, you can't have anything," would be a gross violation of both "notices." In the first place, cleaning a desk area does *not* tell the student what is expected of him. "When you put your books away and pick up the paper," is a much clearer statement. Heaven only knows what, "You can't have anything" means. In the second place, the statement is negative—"If you don't. . . ." It is much more helpful to say, "When you do. . . ."

Turn On (by) the Tape Recorder

Carlos was having a very difficult time in his third grade reading class. According to Mr. Milton's exploratory tests, Carlos was well over a year behind his classmates in reading. He was a very pleasant youngster. He enjoyed playing with his new friends and, for the most part, he always had a broad, warm smile on his face.

Carlos and his family had recently moved to Colorado from Arizona. He had entered Mr. Milton's class in the middle of the term. When Mr. Milton asked Carlos' parents to come to school for a conference, part of Carlos' problem became apparent. Very little English was spoken by either parent, and there was little English written material in Carlos' home. The parents were very cooperative, and they said they would try to help in any way possible.

Mr. Milton believed that with practice, Carlos could make up much of his lost ground in a short period of time. The problem, however, was getting Carlos to practice.

During one of his classes, Mr. Milton announced to his students that later on in the week he was going to bring in a recording made by a famous athlete and, since they were reading about various types of sports, this recorded speech might be very interesting. That Friday, Mr. Milton brought a small cassette tape recorder to class. The youngsters were very excited and, without delay, he turned the set on. For fifteen minutes, the children were fascinated. Most of them knew of the celebrity, and those who didn't found out very quickly. When the speech was over, Mr. Milton placed the cassette on his desk and, for the remainder of the period, he and the students talked about what they had just heard. When the class was over all the students, except Carlos, left the room and went to their next class. Carlos, however, stopped at Mr. Milton's desk and began looking intently at the tape recorder.

"Have you ever seen one before?" Mr. Milton asked.

"No," Carlos responded.

"I will tell you what we can do, if you would like," the teacher began, "why don't you come back after school and I will let you work it." With a big smile, Carlos left for his next class.

For about an hour, Mr. Milton showed Carlos how to use the cassette. Carlos would speak into the recorder and delight in hearing his own voice. While Carlos and Mr. Milton walked off the school grounds together, Mr. Milton promised to bring the tape recorder back to class on Monday.

Mr. Milton quickly realized that one way to help Carlos practice reading was to allow him to use the tape recorder. Not only would it be a reinforcer, but it would also allow Carlos to hear how he was doing.

When Monday came, Mr. Milton had planned some exercises for Carlos. During class, he talked with Carlos about the exercises, and he explained that when Carlos completed his assignments, he would be able to come after school and practice what he had learned in class on the tape recorder. Carlos was very excited about the idea.

For the remainder of the week, Carlos practiced in class and talked to the tape recorder in the afternoon. When Friday came, Carlos was asked if he would like to take the tape recorder home and practice over the weekend. An ecstatic "yes" followed the question.

Mr. Milton wrote a brief note home to Carlos' parents, and he gave Carlos additional assignments to work on. On Monday, Carlos and Mr. Milton would meet after school and, with the book given for the weekend assignment, the two of them would listen to Carlos' progress.

The Premack principle (1965) is very similar to Grandma's rule, although it came from the research laboratory instead of from someone's living room. In essence, it, too, states that a preferred activity can be used as a reinforcer for an activity that is not preferred. Technically it states, "Any high probability behavior (one that occurs very frequently) can be used to increase a low probability behavior (one that rarely occurs)." To use the Premack principle effectively, you allow the low probability behavior to occur first, then the student can engage in the desired high probability behavior. "When you correctly finish your ten math problems, you may go to the library and listen to records," is an example of the principle, assuming the student spends considerable time listening to records and little time working math problems. As with Grandma's rule, one of the advantages of the Premack principle is that the reinforcer the student would like to have is evident from his behavior in class.

It Was Only Meant to Be a Temporary Solution

Mr. Smith's senior honor class was supposedly composed of the school's "brightest" and most "motivated" students. If that was the case, he wondered, why do they seemingly waste so much time? He had developed assignments for them that were labeled intriguing and perplexing, and they were to be challenging as well. Then he remembered that he was the one who had pinned the labels on his topics, not his students.

"I do not know whether you realize it," he began one day in class, "but we waste about half the period getting ourselves ready to do our work. It seems as if you would rather talk with one another than do what I am asking of you. Although you may not agree, some of this 'stuff' is very important. These are issues you will be dealing with in just a few months."

Most of the students appeared embarrassed, having had the "cards" laid on the table. "Until I can figure out what to do," the teacher continued, "I would like to make an agreement with you. The class is one hour long. If you will work hard for forty minutes on my assignments, I will let you continue to work, talk, or whatever you wish to do, within reason."

That is all it took. From that point on, the students did, in fact, work very hard for the forty minutes and often more. Whatever time was left over, the students were given the opportunity to talk about whatever they wished. Mr. Smith never changed his format. If he was asked to join the student conversation, he did. Otherwise, he would leave the room or sit there reading a book. On some occasions, a few of the students would talk with him about what he was reading.

Although some of the other teachers objected to his "permissiveness," he believed his approach to be very productive. He was getting a lot more accomplished, and his students were equally satisfied.

Used cautiously, the approach of allowing a frequent behavior (even a "misbehavior") to take place as a reinforcer for a less frequent behavior can have unexpected benefits.

A Limited Engagement

Duey was the class clown. And, in truth, he was funny. But he was funny at times that weren't very funny, at least to his teacher. His antics were much more frequent than his classroom work. Instead of continuing to warn him, which would only slow him down, the teacher decided to give him the "stage."

"As soon as we finish our spelling, I have a special surprise for you," she announced. "I know there is something all of you would like to do, so as soon as our work is completed, we will do it."

But that was all she said. Duey had no idea what was about to happen. As the teacher predicted, while one of the students was attempting to spell "sinfonietta," Duey let out with one his most popular noises. It was coupled with a "funny" face that had to cause him pain.

Turning to Duey, the teacher said, "My friend, not only are you the surprise, but you are now *on*. Let's go," she said, with a smile, "it's show time!"

Some of his neighbors had to push him to the front of the room, but he got there. However, once up front, he just stood there, squirming. "We are all waiting, aren't we class," the teacher commented.

"Come on, Duey," his friends chided.

Fortunately, his repertoire was limited. One can only make so many noises and so many different faces. When the early laughter turned to silence, Duey quietly took his seat.

On the following day, he once again interrupted class and once again was "asked" to return to the stage. This time his engagement was very brief. His clown act went into mothballs.

In Duey's case it is, perhaps, more accurate to say that his teacher allowed a "forbidden fruit" to occur at will. I have observed teachers use the same approach with very frequent behaviors, often annoying ones, only to find that once given the opportunity, the student's frequent behavior becomes much less frequent. Excessive talking, running around the room, and throwing paper airplanes, are just a few examples.

The Wright Brothers, Revisited

The recent moon landing created an upsurge in the interest in man's flight. The fifth graders had watched the landing on a TV set provided for them in their classroom. For several days afterward, model rockets, spaceships, and airplanes zoomed through the air of the school grounds. Eventually, the latter found their way into Mr. Wright's classroom. Realizing that it would be better in the long run to join the class pilots instead of requiring the "planes" to be grounded, Mr. Wright set up teams in the class, and the students were informed that on completion of their work, airplane races would be allowed during class time.

Participation was purely voluntary. Students who preferred to read or work were allowed to go to the school library and choose the reading material they desired. Students who preferred to watch, instead of "fly" were permitted to do just that. Some of the students were in charge of measuring the distance of the flights, while others assumed the role of "traffic" monitors. The ground rules were simple. Once classroom work was finished, the runways were set up.

The races lasted less than two weeks. As is often the case, when an activity is permitted instead of prohibited, interest diminishes. It was apparent from the students' behavior that not only did they appreciate Mr. Wright, but they were willing to work very hard for him. By associating himself with an activity that was "hot" for the moment, he accomplished a good deal academically, and became a better friend besides.

Summary and Usefulness

This approach can be beneficial to your classroom if you will keep the following points in mind. First, make certain that the behavior you desire and the activity to be used as the reinforcer are both very clear to the students. There should be little question as to what is expected from the students and what will happen as a result of their behavior. Second, always present your description in a positive way. The students, therefore, will know what they must *do,* instead of being told what they must stop doing. Third, you will need an effective reinforcer. What the students say or do can give you some very good ideas about what will be reinforcing. Fourth, require that your desired behavior occurs first, then follow it closely with what the students desire. Fifth, try to be flexible. There is a good chance that a student will continue to try something when he is "prevented" from doing it. Once being allowed to do it, there is an equally good chance he will be less interested in continuing it.

This approach is useful for all grades and ages of students. The basic difference between elementary and senior high school students is in the types of reinforcers. You will find that some of the activities desired by the older students will not be possible, at least given present-day codes for school behavior. I remember giving a presentation to a group of ninth-grade teachers. The art teacher related that her students were not particularly interested in art (painting, etc.), but they were very interested in each other's "physical arts." It was decided that it probably would not be advisable to allow the students to pair off and explore each other, even though that was, according to the teacher, the students' strongest interest.

TEACHER-STUDENT AGREEMENTS

There are a few more formal ways for you to assist students who are having difficulty maintaining their interest in their schoolwork. As you will see, they are more complex than those we have looked at. To help you understand how they work, I will briefly mention something about reinforcement menus, free-time periods, and reinforcement areas. These three topics are often integral parts of the following approaches.

REINFORCEMENT MENUS

You are probably thinking that this topic has something to do with eating at a restaurant. In a kind of far-out sense, it does. Imagine that you and a friend go to a restaurant that you have never tried before. It is Saturday night, a big night for eating out. Yet, as you walk into the restaurant, you see that there is only one other couple seated. You experience a sort of queasy feeling as the other couple looks at you in a way that suggests, "This is not the place to be!" Nevertheless, you are determined to make the best of it. Within a minute, the waiter walks toward your table. You haven't decided what you are going to eat, so you are hoping for a good variety of choices. From a distance, it appears as if the waiter is carrying the menu. As he approaches your table, he smiles, while handing you a three by five index card. Then he hurries back to the kitchen. The card reads, "People have been complaining that restaurants offer too many items to choose from. We have solved that problem. Here you have no choice. We only serve one thing. This *year* we are serving liver. We will serve something different next year. Hope to see you again real soon." (Fat chance!)

You, of course, can get up and leave the restaurant. Now, quickly imagine that you are a youngster in a classroom where the only "reinforcer" offered is the above dish. It's going to be a long year for that youngster. Even if he likes liver, he is going to grow tired of it in a short while. How do you avoid such a situation? Provide the child with a reinforcement menu.

Going Outside and Looking for Bugs

Miss Locke had a unique approach that she used at the beginning of each school year. She would spend several days talking with her students so she could get to know them and they, in turn, could learn something about her. She would tell them what she hoped to accomplish, while asking them what they would like to accomplish during the school year. Usually, by the middle of the first week of school, she made the following statement to her students.

"I am going to do the best I can to make this class interesting and fun. Yes, I did say fun. I will ask you to do some things for me and, in turn, I will try to do some things for you. The very first item on our agenda is for me to find out some of the things that interest you. I do not necessarily mean classroom subjects, but things or activities that you would like to do beyond classwork. Games, activities, hobbies that you enjoy—that's what I would like to know about. I am going to pass out a piece of paper to each of you. On the paper you will see ten lines. I would like you to fill in as many of the ten lines as you wish with things you would like to do. You are in fourth grade now, so I know that there are many fun things you enjoy. If you will share them with me, maybe we will be able to do some of them in class. Okay?"

Miss Locke passed the papers to the entire class. The excitement was evident. One of the boys raised his hand. "Is it okay if we put down something like going on a picnic?" he asked.

"Yes," she answered, "that's just fine."

That evening Miss Locke took the papers home. As expected, there were approximately 200 suggestions. Fortunately, as was also expected, there were over 100 duplications. Of the remaining choices, a few were not practical. One child wanted to visit the moon. Another wanted to go to Disneyland (which was over 3000 miles away; Disney World was not open at the time). Another suggested that he be allowed to stay home and forget school for a couple of years. However, for the most part, the suggestions were practical and administratively feasible. She tallied the remaining list and decided on the twenty-five most popular. Among them were the following:

1. Going on a picnic.
2. Playing with paint.
3. Going to the library to see film strips.
4. Playing games in class.
5. Reading various magazines.
6. Learning to sew.
7. Talking with a neighbor.
8. Talking about hobbies.

In addition to a few more, there were three that were the most popular. One, Miss Locke expected—a visit to the Busch Garden's Zoo. Just about everyone wanted that one. There was another that was a little surprising—a field trip to a 7-11 store. But of all the ones that were submitted, going outside and looking for bugs was the one that floored her. In all the years that she had used the reinforcement menu idea, this one had never been mentioned. However, if some of the kids wanted to do it, it was fine with her—"as long as the bugs are kept in jars," she was to tell them at a later date.

Sometimes you and I think we know what will be reinforcing to our students but, in many cases, we are wrong. Instead of relying on our own opinions, it is just as easy, and usually more accurate, to simply ask the students what they would like to *do* (*not* what they would like to *have*). By doing so, we can obtain a wide variety of activities that can serve as added incentives for classroom behavior. They *do* make the class more fun, and they also help maintain the teacher's social reinforcement.

FREE-TIME PERIODS

Free-time periods not only facilitate learning for many students, they also can be valuable sources of reinforcement. During the free-time periods, students are given the opportunity to explore and experiment with a wide variety of materials and ideas. In some cases, free-time periods are established parts of a student's curriculum. In other instances, free-time periods are made available to a student only after he has successfully completed his assigned work.

Textbooks Are Not the Only Sources of Information

Ames Junior High School had recently completed construction on a new wing of the school's library. The new wing was called the learning center. There was an almost unending supply of materials located in the center. Games, puzzles, tape recorders, audio-visual equipment, typewriters, magazines, newspapers, drawing materials, and a host of other things were made available to the students.

Each teacher was asked to submit to a coordinating committee the times of day he or she would like to use the facilities.

When the room was first opened, Mrs. Jackson took her eighth-grade class to the center so they could see what was available. They were shown the materials and, when necessary, taught how to use them.

During class on the following day, she explained to her students what she desired from them before they would have access to the facilities. Once her class assignments were completed, a student would be given a pass to the learning center. He would be able to stay there until the end of the period. The student could do whatever he wished so long as he did not disturb any of the other students. If a student failed to complete his class assignment, he would not have access to the center for that period. This latter situation was rare, since Mrs. Jackson took great pains to assure that what she asked was within a student's grasp.

The Taj Mahal, It Is Not

When the wind would blow, Boone Elementary School would not only creak, it would sway. This school was so old that the faculty was convinced that Daniel, himself, must have graduated from there.

Unfortunately, there were no plans for renovation or removal. The teachers were hoping for a highly centralized earthquake to hit sometime around midnight on a Saturday. The probability of such was slim.

Blessed with an abundance of ingenuity, Mrs. Hess had developed a "learning center" in the back of her room. She had sectioned off an area by using bookcases and portable closets and her center would comfortably handle about twelve small children. She had supplied the center with whatever she could beg, borrow, or otherwise obtain. She brought magazines from home. Games that were no longer being used by other teachers (or her own children) found their way into the classroom. She requested assistance from the pupils' own parents, and their response, although something less than overwhelming, was helpful. The center was a reasonably fun place to be.

She used the center in two ways. At times, she would assign certain work to the pupils. When the work was finished, the youngsters were allowed to visit the center and enjoy what was available. Quiet behavior was very important, so the children were informed that they would have to leave the area if they became too loud.

At other times, she would have a general class discussion or group presentation and, on completion, she would move one of the portable closets and open the center to all the children at one time. As long as the children were reasonably quiet and shared the materials, they could stay in the center until the next class period.

Although I suspect this next point is obvious, please keep it in mind. It is important that these free-time periods have something to offer the students. There should be many exciting and stimulating materials available. Free time, where few activities exist, can become old very quickly.

Let me call one final point to your attention. Believe it or not, free-time periods and access to learning centers can work against you. Remember, *whichever* behavior earns the student access to free time will probably occur again.

I Think That's Backward

Mrs. Cole had had it. There were two students in her class who were continually causing her trouble. She had talked with them, trying to find out what the problem was. As far as they were concerned, there was no problem. She had threatened them with having to stay after school, but neither the threats nor the occasional detention decreased their disruptiveness. She decided, therefore, to have them leave her class when they failed to behave. The only place she could send them, where there would be some supervision, was the school's learning center. After several days of sending them from the classroom, the two fifth graders were misbehaving more than ever.

Although she did not like having the two youngsters out of the class so often, she was at least able to accomplish something with the remainder of the class when the two boys were not present.

For a while, things were going fairly smoothly with the other pupils. However, in a short time, some of the other students began displaying some highly disruptive behavior. It almost seemed as if the others were copying what the original two boys were doing. Because of the increased disruptiveness, she found herself becoming short tempered. Her frequency of threatened punishment was increasing, yet it was not helping. She began sending more of her students to the learning center when their class behavior was intolerable.

SEVENTEENTH YOUDOIT

Mrs. Cole has a problem. If she doesn't change what she is doing, she is going to find herself teaching very few students. Answer the following questions.

1. What evidence is there suggesting that being sent to the learning center is reinforcing?

   a. _____

   _____

   _____

2. What are the youngsters doing immediately prior to being sent to the center?

   a. _____

3. What would you predict will happen to the frequency of the behavior mentioned in question 2, above?

   increase   decrease

4. You should be ready to handle a fairly complex question. Since I have not defined the term disruptive, you will have to. Once again, think about behavior pairs.

Now, given the information provided in the scene, what would you suggest that Mrs. Cole do to bring about a change in the students' disruptive behavior? (Make certain that your answer deals with increasing a behavior that is incompatible with disruptiveness.)

a. _____

_____

_____

_____

_____

_____

_____

_____

_____

_____

_____

REINFORCEMENT AREAS

Reinforcement areas that are going to be used with any degree of frequency must be convenient for you and your students. If you are teaching in a "self-contained" room, this is your best location. Many of the new "open" schools have activity centers very close to the teaching areas, so the convenience problem is generally solved.

If you do teach in a more or less self-contained area, you might consider sectioning off part of the classroom, usually the back, for your reinforcement area. The noise level in the reinforcement area has to be considered, because there will be times when some students will still be working and excessive noise will most certainly be distracting. On the other hand, the reinforcement area should be a fun (and educational) place to be. Active exploring of provided materials will mean some noise. You will need to determine as best you can how much noise is tolerable. The working students' behavior is, again, your best barometer.

A Most Critical Point

Whenever a positive reinforcement agreement dealing with subject matter (math, reading, etc.) is developed between a teacher and his students, it is absolutely essential that the teacher *know* the students' precise present performance level in that subject area. The present performance level tells the teacher the level of complexity the student is presently able to handle. It tells him how much background information the student brings into the classroom, and thereby decreases the chances that the teacher will ask too much from the student. Without this information, an incentive will rarely benefit a student.

Some of us seem to believe that all that is needed to solve a student's academic problem is to provide massive reinforcement for him. It is not that simple. Imagine your chances of success if I were to offer you an extremely large incentive that you would receive only *after* accurately assembling a jet engine, or *upon* the correct completion of the following "problem":

$$S_p^2 = \frac{\sum_{j=1}^{n_1} (x_{1_j} - \bar{x}_1)^2 + \sum_{j=1}^{n_2} (x_{2_j} - \bar{x}_2)^2 + \sum_{j=1}^{n_3} (x_{3_j} - \bar{x})^2}{n_1 + n_2 + n_3 - 3}$$

There is a better than excellent chance you would never "see" the incentive. In fact, you might not even try for it. Why should you, when the likelihood of receiving it approaches zero?

We will talk about this present performance level measurement and its relationship to skill learning and potential reinforcement in detail when we arrive at the section on skill learning. It is, again, of utmost importance, because it will help you know *where* to begin your teaching program and *where* to set your initial requirements for reinforcement. For the time being, keep in mind that before any reinforcement agreement can be at all successful, the student must have an excellent chance of earning what is made available. Asking him to do something for which he is totally unprepared is like telling *you* that your first or next year's salary depends on your *immediate* answer to the question, "What is a stereotaxic implantation?"

GROUP AGREEMENTS

There are several reasons why reinforcement agreements are made between a teacher and her entire class. First, the agreements bring about a clearer understanding of which behaviors are considered appropriate and inappropriate for that classroom. Second, the agreements help the teacher learn how to reinforce desired behavior and how to "catch the students doing something good." Third, the agreements provide a wide variety of incentives for students to work hard and to follow classroom guidelines. If there is clear communication between the teacher and the students, if the teacher already uses reinforcement effectively, and if the students are already working hard and behaving appropriately, these types of agreements are rarely used.

When considering the use of group agreements, it is necessary that you keep them manageable. If they are too complex and involved, it is unlikely that either you or your students will earn much from them. Therefore, group agreements usually start out with only three or four behavior pairs. Once you and your students find the approach workable, additional behavior pairs can be added.

Let's Get Together a Little Bit

Mrs. Sands was not pleased with the way her class was going. She felt that she could be doing a better job for her students and they could be working a little harder for her. She decided to ask one of her colleagues, whom she believed was an excellent teacher, to give her a hand. The help came in the form of several daily observations of Mrs. Sands' class. The colleague was asked to watch the various ways Mrs. Sands was responding to her students as well as noting the general types of student behaviors that were occurring in the classroom. After a few days, Mrs. Sands and her friend sat together in the teachers' lounge and discussed what had been observed.

"One of the basic problems is the lack of consistency," the friend began. "I think it is pretty difficult for your students to know what you expect of them. One day you seem to want them to do one thing; the next day you don't want them to do it. That is probably confusing to them. And I think the only other major issue is that you seem to be relying almost exclusively on the students' own internal motivation to get them to do their work. A few of them certainly seem to have it, but you have that whole area of students in the back of the room who aren't doing very much. I'm sure you have noticed that you spend some time warning them to do something. If you could change that, I think you'd find the entire class working better together, which should make you feel better, also."

"As hard as it is for me to admit it," Mrs. Sands began, "I think you are right. I have noticed myself yelling more than I care to. I'm certain the children do not like that either."

"Why don't you make a little agreement with them? Talk to them about some of the things you would like them to do and then provide a reason for them to do it. I will help you with the agreement if you'd like."

"Thanks," Mrs. Sands answered, "I would appreciate it."

The First Step: Determining Behavior Pairs

After talking with the class, the following pairs were established.

Desired	*Undesired*
1. Coming to class on time.	1. Coming to class late (without an appropriate reason).
2. Doing class assignments correctly.	2. Not doing class assignments.
	2a. Not doing class assignments correctly.
3. Handing homework in on time.	3. Not handing in homework on time.

"Why the 2a?" the friend asked.

"Well, if they do not correctly complete the assignment, it is, perhaps, partly my fault. My first concern is to have them do the work, then I will worry about accuracy. Does that make sense?"

"It does to me," the friend responded.

The Second Step: Developing the Reinforcement Menu

"What I would like you to do for me," Mrs. Sands began as she stood in front of her class, "is to take a piece of paper and write down any ten things you would like to do while at school. If you'd like, you can get together with some of your friends now and share some ideas. Think about things that would be enjoyable to you, or things you would like to learn or just explore. I can't promise we will be able to do everything you will come up with, but you never know, so put down whatever comes to your mind."

After the youngsters were finished, the papers were passed to the front of the room. That evening, Mrs. Sands took the papers home and selected the twenty-five most popular ideas. She made certain that within the twenty-five choices, some would be very attainable, so the students could have them almost immediately, while some would be more long-range desires.

After a few days, Mrs. Sands posted the following chart on the bulletin board.

Reinforcement Menu

Class Picnic	Playing Charades
Talking With a Neighbor	Extra Recess
Going to the Library	Going to Lunch Early
Painting	Listening to Records
Knitting	Using Typewriter
Reading a Book (student's choice)	Helping Teacher Grade Papers
Reading a Magazine (student's choice)	Playing Catch Outside
	Talking About Sports
Checkers	Talking to Class About Hobby
Sitting Outside on Grass	Field Trip to Airport
Going to the Zoo	Playing Cards in Class
Crossword Puzzles	Drawing Pictures at Desk
Sitting Quietly at Desk and Doing Nothing	Building Model Rockets in Class
	Miscellaneous

"Is the miscellaneous category for some special activity?"

"Yes," Mrs. Sands replied. "I thought that just in case someone came up with something that wasn't on the list, and it was feasible, he should be allowed to do it. Some of these kids come up with interesting ideas."

The Third Step: Assigning Point Values to Behavior Pairs

"Which of your selected behavior pairs are most important to you?" the friend asked.

"I think doing class assignments is most important," Mrs. Sands responded.

"What you might consider doing then, is breaking down the results of the assignments into different levels of accuracy. For example, you might give a higher point value for 90 percent accuracy than for 70 percent accuracy."

"That makes sense," Mrs. Sands answered. "But how do I go about determining the point values?"

"The important thing is to keep in mind that this agreement has to be easy for you to handle," her friend commented. "If you will keep the points low you won't have so much trouble. You wouldn't give a child 273 points for a correct answer—that would drive you buggy in a minute."

"I see what you mean. It's better to give one point for one thing and four or five points for something else."

"Right. Now what you should do is to assign more points for your priority behaviors and less points for the behaviors that aren't that critical," the friend replied.

"What should I do about the undesired behaviors?" Mrs. Sands asked.

"Well, there are two things you can do. First, you can just give plus points for the desired behaviors and do nothing with the undesired behaviors. Or you can give plus points for the desired behaviors and minus points for the undesired behaviors. Personally, I prefer the second approach. Without it, some of the children will have access to the reinforcers even though they haven't done what you really want them to do. If you use the minus points, you will be teaching them what to do as well as what to avoid doing. You will tell your students, of course, that they can avoid the minus points by just doing the few things you are asking. In the long run, that should make things easier for them."

Desired Behavior Pairs with Assigned Points		*Undesired Behavior Pairs with Assigned Points*	
1. Coming to class on time	+1	1. Coming to class late (without an appropriate reason)	-1
2. Doing class assignments		2. Not doing class assignments	-3
a. 90 percent correct	+5		
b. 80 percent correct	+3		
c. 70 percent correct	+1		
d. Improvement over last assignment, but less than 70 percent correct	+1-5[3]		
3. Handing in homework on time		3. Not handing in homework on time	-2
a. Excellent	+3		
b. Satisfactory	+2		

"Now comes the tough part," the friend pointed out. "You must determine how many points will be needed by a student in order for him to have one of the reinforcers on your menu. You should think about this carefully, although you can change the point values if you have accidentally made one too easy or too difficult. If you do change one of them, just be sure to discuss the change with your students. I will give you some guidelines, but you will have to make the final decision based on your own preferences."

"First," the friend continued, "take a look at the point values you have assigned to your behavior pairs. Figure out the *maximum* number of points any one student can earn per day assuming that he comes to class on time; that his class assignments are at least 90 percent correct; and, that he hands his homework in on time and it is excellent."

"Okay," Mrs. Sands responded, "let's see. A student can only come to class on time once per day, so that is plus one. I usually request only one major classroom assignment each day, so if a student completed it with 90 percent accuracy he would earn a maximum of five points. Finally, if a student hands his homework in on time and it is very good, then he could earn an additional three points. Totaling that up, a student could earn nine points per day in my class."

---

[3] Points given depending on amount of improvement.

"I just thought of something," Mrs. Sands continued. "I think this must be important. What happens if a student fails to earn any plus points, or worse, if the student ends up with more minus points than plus points?"

"That is very important," the friend quickly answered. "What you've described may happen. Assuming that your agreement is set up correctly, the student would have to lose out on reinforcement for that day. Think again about your assignment of minus points. They should be sufficient to deter undesired behavior, but not so costly that the student will have a difficult time ending up with positive points. The entire idea of this type of an agreement is that the student gains reinforcement. If the student continually ends up with minus points, then the *system* has *failed*. I remember a colleague who was a little too zealous with her minus points. One of her students, in fact, one of her most disruptive students, ended up with minus 240 points by the end of the first day. Instead of yelling at the student as she had done in the past, each time she noticed that he had done something that was displeasing to her she would say to the student, 'that will cost you ten points.' You can imagine what chance the student had experiencing any of the menu's reinforcement with that many minus points."

"What you are saying, then, is that I must watch the effects of the system very carefully."

"That's right," the friend responded. "If it is not working, if the students are not receiving any reinforcement, then you will have to adjust it. Perhaps your homework assignment wasn't entirely fair. Maybe the students did not have the necessary information to correctly complete the class assignment. That, too, must be considered. Finally, the children may have been tied up in another class so that it was impossible for them to reach your class on time. Oh, one more thing. Although unlikely, the reinforcement menu may need updating. Since you added that miscellaneous category, it's unlikely that the updating will be necessary. But, as you say, you are going to have to watch the effects of the agreement carefully."

"Okay, what's next?" Mrs. Sands asked.

The Fourth Step: Assigning Point Values to the Reinforcement Menu

"Well, now that you know that the students can earn a maximum of nine points per day, the rest is relatively simple. How often would you like your students to have access to their reinforcement menu?"

"Is everyday too often?" Mrs. Sands asked.

"No, not at all. I use it every day, but some teachers prefer every other day, while some use it only once per week. Since your students are young, I would suggest every day, at least in the beginning. You can change this as time passes, but initially, you want your students to quickly see how the system works. You certainly do not want to delay the reinforcement for long periods of time."

"Let's set it up for everyday," Mrs. Sands decided. "As you indicate, I can change it later."

"Fine, now go through your menu and put a mark by the activities that will be easy for you to monitor. For example, an activity that can be done in class on an individual basis would be very easy. On the other hand, an activity that would take a student away from class would be more difficult. And, of course, an activity where all the students leave the class, such as a picnic would, perhaps, be the most difficult for you. You are going to assign very few points to the easy activities, while requiring more points for the difficult activities."

Mrs. Sands looked at her menu. "There are quite a few that will be very easy for me to handle. Painting, knitting, talking with a neighbor, reading a book or magazine, sitting quietly, crossword puzzles, those and others are no problem for me at all. A picnic, field trip, and playing catch will be somewhat more difficult."

"Let me ask you this question," the friend said. "How often would you be able to take the children on a picnic?"

"Once a month would be fun and manageable."

"Okay, how often to the zoo or airport?"

"Maybe once every three or four months."

"Really, all you have to do is decide how often the activities can take place, and then you can determine approximately how many plus points they will require."

"I see what you mean. If I want to take the children on a picnic once a month, or once every four weeks, then I just multiply the number of days times the number of points they can earn—nine—and that figure goes up on the menu."

"That's close, but not quite. Assume that a child can earn forty-five points per week (nine points times five days). If you multiply forty-five by four (four weeks), you would have a total of 180 points. But you can't require the full 180 points for the picnic for two reasons. First, not all of the students are going to earn the maximum points each day. Therefore, some will do very well in your class, but not have enough to go on the picnic, and that's not fair. Second, if you require that every single point goes toward the picnic, the students won't have any points for the smaller reinforcers, and that simply will not work. You would be asking them to go one full month without access to the menu."

"How about if I require fewer points for the picnic?" Mrs. Sands suggested.

"That's exactly right. What you will do is to require a certain number of points for the picnic but still allow the students to have the smaller reinforcers on a daily basis."

"In other words, the students will be able to bank some of their points toward the picnic but still spend some of their points for the daily activities."

"Right, again."

"What I will do, then," Mrs. Sands began, "is to ask each student to bank a minimum of three points per day toward the picnic. Since all the students should be able to earn at least six points per day, that would leave them three points or so for the daily activities. I can see that some of the students will earn enough points for the picnic before some of the others."

"That's okay, all you have to do is to set a date for the picnic well enough ahead so that you give everyone the opportunity to earn the necessary points. If someone earns them well ahead of time you can ask them to serve on the planning committee or something like that."

"I can see a problem with this," Mrs. Sands added. "What happens if some of the students want to go to the zoo while some wish to go on the picnic? I couldn't handle that, I don't think."

"That does happen sometimes," the friend responded. "You either handle it democratically or autocratically. Take a vote and let the majority rule or you decide on the major activity—picnic—and show everyone how much fun it is going to be. This usually isn't a serious problem. You know, our students rarely have the opportunity to do anything like this, so I am certain they will be thrilled to let the majority rule."

"Okay, I believe I have it now. I will operate on the assumption that each student can earn approximately six points per day. Therefore, I will require just a few points for the easy activities and ask them to bank the left over points toward the major activity. If I see that a student is having great difficulty earning the six points, but he is trying very hard, I will adjust the point system to fit him."

"What will you do," the friend asked, "if one of the children does not earn enough points to have even one of the smaller reinforcers?"

"Was he working hard?" Mrs. Sands asked.

"Let's say, no."

"Then he will lose out on reinforcement for that day. He will have to sit quietly in his chair, or I will send him to your room, where he will sit quietly. Hopefully, he will learn very quickly not to lose out on the reinforcement. I believe that the only way for him to learn this is to miss out once or twice, and then he will begin to put out a little more effort."

"And there are a couple of other things I will do," Mrs. Sands continued. "If a student wishes to bank all of his points, that's fine. But once points are banked they can only be spent toward the larger activity. I will do that to prevent a child from having reinforcement one day even though he has not done any of his work. I won't allow him to pull out points from his bank. On the other hand, if a student has been very good and done all his work but he doesn't have enough points to go to the library on Tuesday, he will be allowed to use a few of those earned points toward going to the library on Wednesday, assuming he has also been very good on Wednesday."

Reinforcement Menu with Assigned Points

Class Picnic	+60	Extra Recess	+12
Talking with a Neighbor	+3	Going to Lunch Early	+12
Going to the Library	+6	Listening to Records	+6
Painting	+3	Using Typewriter	+3
Knitting	+3	Helping Teacher Grade Papers	+12
Reading a Book	+2	Playing Catch Outside	+12
Reading a Magazine	+2	Talking about Sports	+3
Checkers	+3	Talking to Class about Hobby	+6
Sitting outside on Grass	+6	Field Trip to Airport	+240
Going to Zoo	+120	Playing Cards at Desk	+3
Crossword Puzzles	+2	Drawing Pictures at Desk	+2
Sitting quietly at Desk	+2	Building Model Rockets	+6
Playing Charades	+12	Miscellanous	

The Fifth Step: Keeping Track of the System

"I think I will purchase a small notebook so I can place the students' names in it and thereby keep a good record of their daily points as well as their banked points. That shouldn't be much of a problem. That way the students can find out how they are doing, if they wish."

The Sixth Step: Reducing the Point System While Keeping the Agreement

"Can I gradually eliminate the points at some time?" Mrs. Sands asked.

"With little difficulty," her friend answered. "Remember, the entire purpose of the agreement is to help you become more consistent, and to help your students know what is expected of them, as well as how you will respond to their desired behavior. Once this is accomplished the points have served their purpose. You, of course, still keep your menu, and the students learn that they still have access to many of the activities as soon as their work is completed. You still can take them on surprise picnics and unexpected visits to the library to see a movie. You still use a good deal of social reinforcement when the students' behavior is desirable. In a sense, very little changes. Free-time periods are provided for the enjoyment of the menu's activities, which is, again, what you had when you used the points."

"So on a given day," Mrs. Sands responded, "I tell the students that no points will be given today but, as soon as their work is completed, they can have one of several activities."

"That should work fine. What you probably want to consider before announcing the change is the types of activities that will be available. On your menu, for example, you probably could allow them any of the activities worth two, three, or even six points. Those are fairly easy activities for you to monitor, don't you think?"

"Should be no problem," Mrs. Sands added. "But what if some of the students still want points?"

"If they are reinforcing to some of the children, then give them. In many cases, points are like grades or notes home to parents. Many students enjoy receiving them, and that's fine. I think what you will find is that once the points are no longer required for certain activities, they will begin to lose some of their reinforcing qualities."

"Should I keep the behavior pairs intact?"

"I certainly would. After all, they are classroom guidelines and I believe you will find that your students will appreciate the very clear information. All teachers have behavior pairs, although they do not call them that. What you are doing is making the behavior pairs known. By doing so, there is less chance for confusion and misunderstanding."

The agreement between Mrs. Sands and her class worked well. As is often the case, there was a tremendous air of excitement when the agreement began. It took the teacher several days to learn to keep track of the points and still present her lesson but, once learned, the system went smoothly. As expected, there were problems. A few of the students began to "bargain" for the activities, even though they had not earned the necessary points. Mrs. Sands, however, simply repeated the rules of the agreement, and the bargaining ceased. In the early stages she found herself reminding some of the students that they would miss out on reinforcement if they failed to earn their points, but she stopped this practice when she realized this might be reinforcing for some and threatening to others. Instead, she relied on the agreement, and most of the students just started working harder to earn the necessary points.

Almost immediately, she observed an increase in student productivity. Homework was coming in on time, and its accuracy was better than ever. Class assignments were being completed by students who had done very little in the past. She also noticed a significant reduction of warning and threatening on her part. The class atmosphere had changed and it was a very pleasant place to be.

Summary and Usefulness

For group agreements to be successful, they must be clear and they must be reasonable. The students should know what is expected of them, and they are more likely to know this when the decided behavior pairs are observable and thoroughly discussed. The reinforcers used in these agreements should be varied, and the students should be involved in their selection. Finally, try to keep the delay between appropriate behavior and enjoyment of the reinforcers to a minimum. The points used in the agreement will help decrease the delay, particularly when they are used along with your social reinforcement.

These systems are easier to use with younger students primarily because of the ease with which various reinforcers can be found. However, with some modification, group agreements can be effective with high school students as well. In place of points, high school teachers have used records of student performance, such as test grades or accuracy of assignments, to determine which activities will be made available to the students. The reinforcement menu is determined almost solely by the students, with the teacher, perhaps, making the final decision regarding the feasibility of the students' suggestions.

These types of incentive agreements are time consuming and initially, at least, cumbersome. With practice, however, they are not that difficult to manage, and they very often produce dramatic positive changes in classroom behavior. As Dr. Bushell points out (1973), "Perhaps the biggest return for the effort comes from the virtual elimination of management problems which lead to hassles, commands, threats, and punishment."

Remember, you can start out small. You can select one or two behavior pairs to work with; you can develop an abbreviated reinforcement menu; and your points can be given out within a half-hour period. What you will probably find is that your students' excitement will be reinforcing to *you*, and you will gradually increase the system's complexity.

INDIVIDUAL AGREEMENTS BETWEEN TEACHER AND STUDENT

If you become disappointed with the work of only one or two students and not the entire class, you can modify the above system to fit the needs of the few students. These agreements can also deal with social and academic areas.

As with the group agreements, individual agreements must specify two things. First, what work (or behavior) must take place. Second, what will happen as a result of the completion of the work. Every effort should be made to involve the student in the determination of the desired work and resulting reinforcer, because the student is more likely to cooperate if he has had something to say about the agreement.

Lost In a Crowd

Prior to fifth grade, Robert was doing very well in school. This year, however, he was having great difficulty with math, reading, and spelling. Conversation with Robert, his teacher, and his parents failed to offer any information that might explain Robert's lack of effort. He was a very nice youngster who rarely got into any social difficulty. He had many friends, and he appeared to enjoy a good relationship with most everyone.

The school psychologist decided to visit Robert's room to see if she could uncover some information that might be used to help him. On the initial day of observation, she encountered her first problem—she couldn't find Robert. Although the teacher knew he was in class, she couldn't find him either.

The class was a modified open classroom. In other words, the school decided to knock some walls down to produce a more open atmosphere. There were ninety students in the area, with two teachers and one aide. The same teacher was responsible for the three subjects with which Robert was having difficulty, as well as social studies, which for some curious reason, was little problem to Robert. In fact, according to the teacher, Robert was one of the best students she had in social studies.

Quite obviously, the first task the teacher and school psychologist had was to locate the youngster. After a few minutes, they found him neatly tucked away behind some bookcases. Three of his friends were there with him. They were playing Scrabble.

"This class just isn't any fun," Robert confided to the school psychologist. "Besides, I never see the teacher. She's nice and everything, but I'd rather sit in the corner. I don't think she minds. . .she hasn't said anything about it, anyway."

"But you are doing so well in social studies. How come?"

"That's different. Most of the time we go to the library. . .read some newspapers and stuff. That's fun. It's quiet in there. . .noisy in here."

He was absolutely correct about the noise level. Between the hard wood floor, the fairly high ceiling, the eighty-nine other students, and the bare walls, it was like being at a Rock concert with your ear placed next to an amplifier.

"Would you like to spend a little more time in the library?" the psychologist asked.

"You mean today?"

"Today and other days, too, if you would like."

"Far out," Robert said with a smile. (The "old" psychologist correctly interpreted Robert's enthusiastic response.)

"Let me talk with your teacher and I will be back to see you in a while," she explained.

Robert's teacher was willing to try almost anything that would benefit him. She agreed with the psychologist that using the library as a reinforcement area was worth a try. She decided, therefore, to set up an agreement with Robert. The agreement would stipulate various a-mounts of work and various amounts of free time that could be earned as soon as the work was completed. The teacher, school psychologist, and Robert met that afternoon to discuss the agreement.

"You will be able to spend anywhere from one to thirty minutes in the library almost every day. The only exception will be if we have a class project where we are all doing something together. How much time you spend in the library is entirely up to you. Okay, so far?"

"Yes, ma'am," Robert answered. "Can I do anything I want?"

"As long as you are quiet and do not disturb anyone."

"Far. . ., I mean, Yes, ma'am."

"You will be able to earn up to ten minutes for your math work, ten minutes for your spelling, and ten minutes for your reading. What I will do is to give you a piece of paper each morning when you come to school. On the paper you will find several assignments for each subject area. You will see that the more work you do, the more time you will be able to earn. Again, it will be your choice as to how much you wish to do."

"What happens if I do not finish the work?" Robert asked.

"Well, first of all you will only be asked to do what I am reasonably certain you can do. Of course, some of the work will be more difficult than other work but, if you apply yourself, you should be able to do the harder work. However, if you do not finish the work, then you will not earn the maximum amount of time for the library. I have complete records of what you have been doing in the three subject areas, so what I will ask you to do will be fair. I will also tell you exactly how many pages, problems, or words you must work on and exactly how much time you will earn by doing two, four, six, eight, or ten problems."

"So if I do six problems, I can earn more time than if I only do four problems?"

"That's right. By reading eight pages and answering the questions, you will earn more time than if you only read four pages and answer those questions," the teacher responded. "All I will ask you to do is to decide in the morning what you would like to do for the day. What you decide will be the minimum amount you will do. Of course, you can decide to do more at any time if you wish."

As the teacher indicated, each morning Robert was presented with a piece of paper explaining what had to be done for the day. Robert read over the assignments and selected how many problems, pages, and words to work on. When he completed his work he brought the agreement sheet and the finished work to the teacher's desk. The work was checked, and Robert was given a note to be handed to the librarian, indicating when Robert had to return to class.

For the first three days, there were virtually no problems. Robert did the amount of work he chose to do and went to the library for the amount of time agreed on. On the fourth day, however, something unexpected happened. One of Robert's closest friends and fellow Scrabble players came to the teacher and asked if he could have a similar agreement. It was apparent that he and Robert had discussed the agreement because he had a written agreement ready to hand the teacher. Somewhat taken aback, the teacher asked for a few minutes to consider the second youngster's request.

"If the librarian has no objections," the psychologist suggested, "I think you should go ahead and set up an agreement with Mike, also. After all, you can't very well allow only one student access to the reinforcement area. That just isn't fair. If Mike functions better under this system, then we should be flexible."

"I am a little apprehensive about allowing the two of them to be in the library at the same time. Jane (the librarian) might shoot me."

"Okay, I'll tell you what. Set the agreement up and I will watch the two of them without them knowing it. If they start horsing around, I will just inform them that they will lose the library privileges unless they are reasonably quiet," the school psychologist said.

The two boys did not create any problem whatsoever. Several observations showed the same thing—they sat quietly together looking at magazines. On one occasion, they were found doing a crossword puzzle. On another, they were playing Scrabble. On a third, they had a world map laid out on a table. According to the psychologist, it sounded as if the boys were planning their summer vacation to Africa.

Summary and Usefulness

As long as a teacher has an accurate estimate of the student's present performance level, individual agreements can be very beneficial to students. All that needs to be done is the careful determination of what work is expected and what incentive will be provided. Again, it is necessary that the agreement be very clear. Knowing how many problems, how many pages, and how many words are to be completed decreases the chances for confusion and uncertainty. In addition, by allowing a student to have more reinforcement for more work, the teacher builds in an added incentive for the student to work harder.

Be aware that there are potential problems with this type of an approach. Once a good thing gets going, word travels quickly. Mike heard about the agreement and he wanted to be included. As it turned out, no other student wished to accompany Mike and Robert. But there will be times when other students will want to be involved. On the surface, that may not appear to present much of a problem. However, if a student finds that the *only* way he can be included in the "special" program is to *misbehave* or do very little work, he may just do that. To avoid this, many teachers give their entire class the option to have such agreements. In this way, the "good" student is not penalized for being good.

M & M's and a Bag Full of Trouble

After hearing a brief inservice presentation on teaching strategies, Miss White thought she had the answer to her problem. (Unfortunately, she hadn't listened carefully to what was said.) When she returned to class, she quietly called Mary to her desk.

"Mary, you have not been doing your assignments lately, and I know that you can do them. To help you along, I have decided to give you a few M & M's as soon as you complete the twenty multiplication problems. Bring your paper up to my desk when you are finished. If they are correct I will give you the candy. You will have to eat them in the hallway and I want you to promise me that you won't tell any of the other children. Okay?"

"You betcha!"

Mary completed her work in record time. She happily skipped to Miss White's desk, where she was greeted with a smile. "I knew you could do it," accompanied the smile. "Let's go out to the hallway, and you can have your treat."

Sometimes promises are pretty difficult to keep. Although Mary did not use a megaphone she, nevertheless, was able to communicate to her friends what had happened before many minutes had passed.

"That's not fair," shot up from the back of the room. "Waaaaait a second," immediately followed. "How come?" echoed off the walls. The class leader, spokesman, and general good fellow raised his hand and was immediately recognized by the now thoroughly shaken teacher.

"In my estimation," the precocious youngster began, as if speaking to the Supreme Court, "there has been an accidental miscarriage...an inequity, so to say. Most of us have been doing our work all along, yet I do not recall any such treats being passed into our hands. That ain't fair!"

"Yikes," the teacher thought to herself. "My apologies to you all," she announced. "I guess the only appropriate thing I can do now is to offer all of you who have completed your work a few M & M's. Is that fair?"

"More than fair," the spokesman commented. And a sigh of relief could be heard by all.

Miss Martin

"I hate to be a nag, but something about these last two approaches concerns me. I like the idea behind them, particularly because they appear to have helped the students. But the fact that they *have helped* is my concern."

"What is going to happen to Mike and Robert when they go to sixth grade? In fact, what is going to happen with all of Mrs. Sands' students when they leave her room? Won't they want to be treated in the same way next year? Won't they expect the same kind of approach? It seems as if they are all being set up for a big disappointment."

"Maybe they will be lucky and have you for a teacher," the speaker warmly responded.

"I'm being serious," Miss Martin stated.

"But so am I," the speaker quickly answered. "With any kind of good fortune, the next teacher in line will work as hard for her students as Mrs. Sands and Robert's teacher did."

"And if they are not so fortunate?"

"Then the youngsters will not only be disappointed, they will probably lose out a little academically."

"That bothers me."

"That bothers me also," the speaker commented. "If it can be shown that some youngsters work harder and enjoy school more under an agreement-type system, why not use it? Aren't schools systems ideally set up to meet the needs of students? Or is it the other way around—the students are supposed to meet the needs of the school system?"

"Maybe it would have been better if the students had never experienced the agreements that were used," Miss Martin pondered out loud.

"Better for whom?" the speaker asked rhetorically. "Certainly not for the students. Let's ask them. Let's ask them if they enjoyed school during that period. Let's ask them if they learned a good deal. What will we say if their answer is 'yes' to both questions? What will we say to their parents? What will we say to ourselves?"

"I feel like I am on a merry-go-round," a young man said emotionally from the side of the auditorium. "Here we are saying that a teacher has the power to select an approach. If there is one that he doesn't like, or one that would require 'too much' of his time, regardless of its potential effects for his students, then that's that. I have a youngster in school now. He's not a genius, but he's not a dummy either. He doesn't work that hard in class. He tells me there are other things he would rather do. His work, as a result, is only average. Am I supposed to accept the idea that his work will always be only average? I wonder what would happen if his teacher would try one of these ideas we've just heard? I can't help but think that a little incentive would help him a great deal. I'm just sure of it."

The auditorium was silent. The speaker quietly looked around the room.

"Have you talked with his teacher?" one of his colleagues asked.

"As a matter of fact, I have," the young man said. Still upset, he turned toward Miss Martin. "Do you know what he said to me? He told me that he has thirty-two students in his class, not just one or two!"

INDIVIDUAL AGREEMENTS BETWEEN TEACHER, STUDENT, AND PARENT

Sometimes, it is difficult for teachers to develop agreements for their students. The class may be very large. There may be no activity center, or the library may be small and crowded most of the time. Even the classroom itself may be too small to contain an effective reinforcement area. Aside from the philosophical and "moral" issues of reinforcement, a major difficulty teachers often have with group and individual agreements is the administration of the reinforcement component. Without minimal types of facilities or without cooperation of other teachers, supervising earned reinforcement can pose problems. There is, however, a viable alternative, assuming a student's parents are willing to cooperate, which should be considered if some of the above problems exist.

These types of agreements, again, require a clear statement as to the level and quantity of work expected from the student. (Knowledge of the student's present performance level is also required.) The student is either assigned, or chooses on his own, daily exercises, and the teacher keeps a record of the student's performance. The student is then awarded a certain number of points for his completed work. A record of the earned points is taken home to the parents, and activities are selected from a home-developed reinforcement menu. In most cases, the parent will need considerable help from the teacher in developing this menu, particularly in the area of assigning point values to the various activities. The student also helps his parents develop the menu. By doing so, there is a better chance that the menu will contain reinforcers desired by the student.

A Teacher's Aide—Parents

The phone call came early in the morning. It was apparent that the woman was having difficulty holding back her tears.

"I just don't know what we are going to do," she began. "Amy refuses to do any work at school. This is so new to us. . .she's always done so well. I'm sorry that I'm so upset. I know you have better things to do than to listen to a crying mother."

After a few more minutes, the psychologist suggested that the mother and father come to his office to discuss the matter, to which the mother immediately agreed.

"I think we have been lazy," Father said. "For the last three years or so we haven't been very involved with Amy's school. We're interested, of course, but we have pretty much relied on the school to take care of everything. Her grades have always been good. Her teachers have never mentioned anything about problems. I guess we just assumed that everything was fine."

"Jack's right," Mother added. "Before three weeks ago I never would have dreamed that this would happen. It seems like all of a sudden she's changed." As her voice tapered off, the tears swelled in her eyes. Immediately her husband took her hand and then looked in the direction of the man seated behind the desk.

"Have you discussed the problem with the teacher?" the psychologist asked, after assuring the mother that he would try to assist in every way.

"We had a discussion yesterday," Father answered, "but nothing was resolved. Amy's teacher is as confused as we are. She did say, however, that she would help in any way. As a matter of fact, she gave us your name."

"Why did this happen?" Mother asked. "Why now?"

"I would like to be able to tell you," the psychologist answered, "but anything I would say would only be a guess. Why don't we talk with Amy's teacher? Maybe we will find something out. The truth is that we may never know the 'why,' but that doesn't mean that we can't work with the situation. Try to be patient for awhile. I am certain we can do something."

A conference was set up the following afternoon. As the parents indicated, the teacher was at a loss as to why Amy was not working. It was pointed out, however, that the class was very large and this was, perhaps, an important variable. The teacher did not hesitate to admit her dissatisfaction with the class arrangement. Because of decreasing enrollment, one of her fellow teacher's contract was not renewed, and Amy's teacher was given an additional six students. The size of the class made it very difficult to respond to each child on an individual basis.

"What really upsets me," the teacher began, "is the fact that I know that I am not getting to all the children. To be honest, I am almost afraid to find out how many students I am missing. I do not remember ever being this frustrated with my job. Something must be done. We have a Parent Teacher Organization meeting coming up soon, and I hope to be able to get some of the parents to help me out."

"I talked with Amy this morning, knowing we were meeting today and I didn't get much from her," the teacher continued. Then she looked at Amy's mother and asked, "Has she told you anything?"

"Not much, except she assures us that she will try harder and that she likes you."

"I like her, too. I like all the kids. They are really nice. It almost kills me not to have the time to touch each one of them. I dare anyone to tell me that we have too many teachers these days. Boy, could I use at least one of them. In fact, I could find a job for each of the so-called surplus teachers."

After a few moments of silence, the teacher said, "I'm sorry, I didn't mean to jump on my soap box now. " Looking toward the parents she added, "We'll work out something for Amy, I promise you."

"Could the work be too hard for her?" Father asked, breaking a few more minutes of silence.

"I thought about that," the teacher answered, "but I just do not think that's it. When I met with Amy earlier, I quizzed her on the information that she was supposed to have done yesterday, which, unfortunately, she didn't do. Sitting across from me, she did fine. I was very pleased. I was hoping that she would have been pleased also, but I don't think she was. I just do not know. . .maybe what we are learning is boring. . .I just do not know."

"Why don't we try a little home agreement?" the psychologist suggested. "It might just work," he added.

"That's fine with me," the teacher responded.

"I'm not certain what it is," Father said.

"Well, a home agreement is a way for us to provide Amy with some incentive to work a little harder in class. I'm certain she will find it agreeable and it might be just what we all need. When we set it up, I will sit down with Amy and see what she thinks about it. Let me tell you exactly what we are going to do," he continued. "First, we have to make a decision about what we want Amy to do in class, the types of work and the quantity and quality. The amount of work will be reasonable, and it will be within Amy's grasp. Second, we will need to develop a list of incentives for Amy to work for."

"That should be very easy," Mother quickly interjected. "She loves to stay up late on weekends."

"Don't forget McDonalds," Father added. "That seems to be the most important thing to her these days. French fries and a Coke; I think she is going to turn in to a french fry one of these days."

"That's great," the psychologist commented. "We should also talk with Amy to see if there is anything else, within reason, that she would like."

"She does like to watch television and sometimes read," Mother added.

"Fine. Now, the third thing we will need is a means of communication between the teacher and yourselves. The easiest way for us to develop this is through the use of a chart that Amy will bring home each school day. The chart will indicate how Amy did that day and, based on her performance, she will be able to select one of the various reinforcers."

"That's like a point system, isn't it?" Mother asked.

"Yes, it is. Amy will earn a certain number of points for her work in school, and then she will spend the earned points as she desires at home. This helps the teacher considerably, because the responsibility for reinforcement falls on your shoulders."

"That's fine with us," Mother added. "We would like to become more involved."

"What I will do each morning," the teacher began," is present Amy with a choice of things for her to do during my class hours with her. She will be able to earn more points for more work and, in that way, earn more reinforcement. I will add up the points earned for that day and write the number down on the chart. For example, five points for math, seven for reading, and three for spelling. All of the points will be entered under the appropriate day (Monday, Tuesday, etc.). If you do not mind, I would like you to sign it, so when she brings it to me the next morning I will know that you have seen it."

"Certainly," Father said.

"We will help you set up the list of incentives and the points needed for each of them, but remember that Amy can only have the reinforcers after she has earned the necessary points. Additionally, she doesn't have to spend any of them. She can bank them for one of the larger reinforcers, such as a book or movie," the psychologist added.

"How long should we continue with the agreement?" Mother asked. "That is pretty hard to answer right now. Let's try it for a couple of weeks and see what happens. Amy will have the option to stop the system anytime she wishes. If she continues to do her work without the agreement, she still will have access to various special reinforcers, but on a very informal basis. However, if she fails to do her work, she will have to forfeit some of her desired activities for a brief period of time."

Amy was pleased with the agreement. However, she accomplished very little work during the first few days. Her performance did increase noticeably by the end of the week, and she quickly learned what would happen as a result of her work and absence of work. The agreement stayed in effect for four weeks, at which time the points were discontinued and replaced by an occasional note from the teacher to Amy's parents. Three months after the agreement was formally dropped, Amy was still doing well in school. One possible reason for this was that her parents were not only very interested in her schoolwork, but they did not hesitate to demonstrate their appreciation of her effort.

Summary and Usefulness

With the increasing numbers of students being assigned to an individual teacher (or team teachers), it is often difficult to provide a variety of in-class incentives. In the event that the "natural" incentives, such as exciting presentations, novel materials, and different enjoyable activities, fails to "turn on" a few students, a teacher can use a home agreement to help herself and her students. The necessary ingredient, of course, is the cooperation of the parents.

My experience suggests that the home agreements have a more positive effect with elementary and junior high students than senior high students. This is due to the observation that many of the incentives desired by the older student are often out of the financial range of most parents. However, staying out later on weekends, having an opportunity to help plan family outings, and more freedom to choose special activities, such as Rock concerts, are often practical incentives desired by the older student. Home agreements built around these and other valued activities have proven successful for the senior high student.

THE INCORRECT USE OF INCENTIVES

Artificial incentives and agreements will *never* take the place of a good teacher. Even the most powerful reinforcer will be of little help if the entire school day is boring, tedious, and unwelcomed. Artificial incentives accompany good teachers. They are used in conjunction with an exciting school atmosphere. They are used to help desired behavior get started so the more natural incentives can take over. When used correctly, they can assist teachers tremendously. However, when used *incorrectly,* they can have a devastating effect on a youngster.

A Badge That Should Have Been, but Wasn't

One can only guess what the total effect of the incident had on David. To be certain, it had its effect, for the disappointment was reflected in David's behavior for several weeks.

Although David was beset with physical problems, he nevertheless had an amazing capacity to fight back. This was, perhaps, one of his toughest fights of his young life.

David was an exceptionally frail youngster. He had had numerous illnesses, each of which had taken its toll on his physical strength. At eight years of age, he was unable to keep up with his peers, particularly on the playground. His friends seemed to know this and, for the most part, they helped and supported his efforts. Sadly, his physical education teacher wasn't as knowledgeable.

The winter season prevented the children from playing outside, so the indoor physical education activities were mostly basketball, various running games in the gym, and gymnastics. During one particular week the major activity was rope climbing. David was in a class with twelve other youngsters. Their teacher decided to provide the children with an incentive to climb the rope to its highest point. The announcement was made that once having reached the knot at the top part of the rope, a student would receive a badge declaring his proficiency. In turn, the badge would be placed on a bulletin board in the gym for all to see.

Each child took his turn. The task was relatively simple—for most of the youngsters. Some climbed the rope within seconds, while others took several straining minutes to reach the top. David, however, was not so fortunate. He progressed no further than about fifteen inches. He was able to move his right hand "over" his left only three times. His legs were of little assistance, since they were equally weak. His friends yelled their encouragement, but their voices did not make the knot attainable. David's expression was painful. His muscles twitched under the strain. He eventually stopped trying and fell to the mat under the rope. With no assistance, he picked himself up and walked to the back of the line. All he could do was to sit down on the floor. A consoling pat on his shoulder earned one of his friends a weak smile.

David did not receive a badge. His name was the only one not placed on the bulletin board. He had tried! In fact, he had *improved* over his previous attempt. But he did not receive a badge. It was hard for him to understand. His parents' initial reaction was anger (as was mine). After a short time, when the feelings cooled off, Father proceeded to fashion David a badge, which was hung in his room. A letter was sent to the physical education teacher, but there was no reply.

David will make it despite the incident, but. . . .

It Could Be You in That Seat

The class and I had just completed our discussion on the importance of considering the child when developing classroom behavior pairs. As a part of our final project, the students were asked to spend several days observing teachers in their classrooms. One of the objectives for the students was to compile lists of behavior pairs presently being used and then ask the teachers if they were aware of the pairs they were enforcing.

Several days after the assignment began, one of the members of the class came into my office. Noticeably upset, she related the following account.

She encountered a first-grade teacher who was offering her pupils an opportunity to earn some M & M's. To receive them, the youngsters were asked to do something that on the surface, might seem reasonable—sit quietly in their seats. However, they were required to sit in their seats without moving. They had to be perfectly immobile. They were required to sit that way for a full ten minutes. No movement, no conversation, no fidgeting, no nothing for ten minutes! The teacher sat in the front of the room so she could watch each child. To make matters worse, she had informed the children that if one child "misbehaved," no one would receive any candy. The student teacher, observing from the back of the room, noticed that one of the children was crying. At the same time, she noticed that the child was trying very hard to hold back the tears for fear that an outburst would cause her classmates to lose out on the "treat." The teacher was apparently satisfied with the quiet behavior, since she passed out a few pieces of candy to each child. Not too surprising was the student teacher's observation that the children did not appear to enjoy what they had received.

Back in my office, the student teacher told me that had she been a child in one of those seats, she would have told the teacher what she could do with the M & M's!

It goes without saying that there will always be a few who misuse suggested ideas. Hopefully, you will not be one of them. Before you consider incentives and agreements, think about what you are doing. Consider the behaviors you will be requesting. Are they appropriate, reasonable, *and* beneficial to the student? Remember, it could be you in that classroom seat. How would you react to what was being asked?

WORKING TO AVOID PUNISHMENT

"My feeling is that we, his teachers, have to provide him with a reason to start learning; to become interested in something. If we don't, who will?"

"I never thought about it," Miss Martin answered.

"Well, my dear, we'd better start thinking about it. You know, if we fail to provide him with something positive to work *for*, we are going to end up providing him with something 'unpleasant' to work to avoid, such as, our punishment."

"I'm not certain that I understand that," Miss Martin said.

"You will in just awhile," Anne responded. (From p. 57)

"Most of us are pretty lazy," Anne continued. "We have found that it is much easier to get students to do certain things by threatening them with some form of punishment. Many of our students do, in fact, accomplish what we want because they have learned that by doing so, they can *avoid* our punishment."

"How about an example?" Miss Martin requested.

"Okay, suppose you are observing a second-grade teacher. You notice that the teacher tells the youngsters that as soon as they complete their reading assignment, they can go outside and have a few extra minutes of recess. You see that the children quickly finish their work and, as promised, they are allowed to leave class and join some of their friends who are outside playing. How would you characterize the teacher's approach?"

"That sounds pretty positive," Miss Martin answered. "The students were given the opportunity to earn something pleasant for their work."

"I would agree with you," Anne responded. "Now, suppose you are observing another teacher with the same age group. You hear the teacher tell the students that they will *lose* their recess period if they *fail* to complete their work. You notice that these youngsters also finish their work quickly."

"That's a negative approach, isn't it? In this second case, the youngsters were working hard to *avoid* losing their recess period," Miss Martin responded.

"Right. Whenever we threaten a student with some form of punishment to get him to do something, it's most certainly a negative approach. We all probably do this frequently. Instead of praising a student when he does raise his hand, we threaten him with punishment if he doesn't raise his hand. Instead of thanking a student for his homework, we tell him what will happen if he doesn't hand it in. We warn him that he will have to stay after school if he misbehaves, while providing him with little when he behaves as we wish."

"That's what happens when we drive a car," another teacher suggested. "We know what will happen when we exceed the speed limit, so to avoid the ticket we usually drive within the speed limit."

"We do as long as there is a policeman around," added another teacher.

"You have just hit one of the problems with this negative approach right on the button," the speaker quickly interjected. "Have you ever noticed what happens in a classroom when the source of the threatening and punishing is no longer around?"

"Boom—the place explodes," was heard from the back of the auditorium.

"As a matter of fact," still another teacher commented, "I remember a similar situation in one of my college classes. The teacher was a real bore. He was never prepared; his class was almost useless. Given a choice, I doubt that many of us would have attended. But, if we missed his class he would deduct points toward our final grade. So we went to his sh---y class to avoid losing the points. When he would cancel class, we were thrilled. We didn't lose the points, and we didn't have to listen to him, either. Given the circumstances, that was about the best of all possible worlds."

"We must have had the same teacher," Anne responded laughing. "But you know, there is something else about this negative approach that some of us fail to realize. In order for it to be at all effective, we have to have something the student wishes to *avoid*. I know of a situation when a teacher told a student that if he failed to study for her class she was going to give him an F for his final grade. You know what his response was? 'Go ahead,' he said, 'I've got three of them already. One more won't bother me.' "

"I hate to admit it," Miss Martin said, "but I think I have been doing this very thing with one of the boys in my class. I keep telling him that he is going to stay after school if he continues to be disruptive."

"Is he still as disruptive?" Anne asked.

"As a matter of fact, yes."

"Do you keep him after school?"

"Not all the time."

"In other words, you threaten him with something *you* think is punishing, but you do not always carry through with it, right?"

"You've just mentioned two more problems with the approach," the speaker once again interjected. "First, if you are going to threaten punishment, you must have something that is punishing to the student, not something you think is punishing. Second, if you threaten, but do not carry through, the student will quickly learn that you do not mean what you say, so your threat is weakened."

"Are there other problems?"

"Several," the speaker commented. "Let me give you a little help by offering you another key."

KEY:	Any behavior that enables a student to avoid punishment will occur again in the future. The behavior that increases is the one that allows him to avoid the punishing situation.

"Students often learn to avoid punishment by doing what is required or asked of them. They find out that by sitting quietly they are not scolded. They discover that they can avoid a poor grade by handing in their assignments. They realize that one way to avoid being sent to the principal's office is to avoid misbehaving in class, or behave as the teacher desires."

"Excuse me, but couldn't you get the same things through the more positive approach?" a teacher asked.

"Most definitely. You could provide an incentive for the students to sit quietly, complete their assignments, and behave appropriately in class if these are some of the things desired of them. My preference, of course, is to use the positive approach whenever possible. You will see the reason why when we look at some of the potential side-effects of punishment. But the reality of today's school situation suggests two things. One, some teachers are going to use the threat of punishment to increase behavior regardless of advice to the contrary, and two, some students appear to be more affected by the threatened punishment than by the occasional use of social or even material reinforcement."

"Then you are saying that there are times, with some students, when the threat of punishment is appropriate."

"Well, I'm saying that at times, with some students, the threat of punishment does bring about desired behavior. For example, I've experienced a situation where a student was informed that he would be asked to leave school for a period of time if he continued to be highly aggressive. Apparently, the threat of such punishment was very meaningful to him, because he abruptly stopped his fighting. I've known teachers who have tried to rely exclusively on a positive approach only to find that the desired behavior simply did not occur. However, when the class was informed that their continued disruptiveness would result in the loss of a desired activity, the appropriate behavior began almost immediately. Once the desired behavior occurred, the teacher went back to his more positive approach."

"He used a combined approach, then."

"Right. Once the students began to behave in order to avoid the punishment, the teacher used positive reinforcement to influence the desired behavior. If the teacher had consistently used the negative approach without the positive approach, he would have eventually found himself in trouble."

"Look at it this way," the speaker continued. "How would you react or feel if your behavior for an entire school day was being influenced by threats of punishment? That the very best you could obtain from school was the avoidance of unpleasant consequences?"

"I could only stand so much of that," Miss Martin volunteered. "It would be horrible."

"What would you do?" the speaker persisted

"I believe I would try to leave," she answered.

"I would stay and fight back," another stated.

"I don't think I would learn very much—or at least want to learn very much," still a third suggested.

"I'd drop out," a fourth offered. "Maybe not physically, but certainly mentally. Come to think of it, I might just drop out physically."

"Everything that all of you have just said," the speaker continued, "probably happens more times than we know. Despite these very possible outcomes, we use the threatening approach frequently because it does work, at least for the moment. We actually get reinforced for using it. We find that our unexpected threat brings a halt to an undesired behavior. As a result, we use it again. But we rarely look at the full ramifications of our actions. Instead, we are satisfied with the momentary results."

"Most of us sitting here know that in order for our threat to be at all effective, the source of the threat, usually the teacher, must be present. We know, too, that before the threat will be meaningful to the student, what is threatened must be seen as a form of punishment by the student. Finally, most of us know that if the threat is made and the desired behavior does *not* occur, the threat must be carried out. But what most of us do not know is that once a teacher carries through with his threat and actually applies his punishment, he enters a whole new ball game, and a host of new problems have to be considered. In the long run, these new problems are going to nullify the momentary 'positive' gains observed when the threat initially worked. All the things you just mentioned, the leaving, the fighting back, the lack of interest in learning, the physical and mental dropping out, come to the foreground and smack us right in the face."

"I am beginning to understand what Anne meant," Miss Martin reflected, "when she suggested that we'd better start thinking about the positive approach."

Teaching
Students
What Not
To Do

Knowing what not to do is about as informative as being told by a gas station attendant, after having asked him for directions, "I'm sorry, but you *can't get there from here.*

If a student knows *what not to do* he can at times, by inactivity, avoid punishment and other displeasures. But he can stay inactive for only so long. Sooner or later he is going to try something and, if he doesn't know *what to do,* he is right back in the same situation. Therefore, let it be known at the beginning of this section that if you, as the teacher, do accomplish what the above title suggests, you haven't accomplished very much!!

Teacher: Johnny, how many are two and two?

Johnny: Five!

Teacher: Wrong! Try again.

Johnny: (Well, at least I know *not* to say five.) How about six?

Teacher: Wrong again, John! Try again, John! Think, John!

>*Johnny:*   (This is getting ridiculous. I know not to say five and not to say six. I'll try once more and that's it.) Three? Wrong again?
>
>*Teacher:*   Wrong again!

We are going to look at some ideas that can be used to decrease the occurrence of various behaviors. By themselves, the ideas are not very effective aids. They only show a student what not to do. They do not teach him what to do. If you rely on them exclusively to deal with classroom behavior problems, before very long you will find that a great percentage of your teaching day will be devoted to an exhausting contest in which there are no winners.

BEHAVIOR PAIRS: THE KEY TO TEACHING STUDENTS WHAT TO DO AND WHAT NOT TO DO

Many of us have fallen into a habit of not paying any attention to desirable behavior while reacting quite harshly to annoying and bothersome behaviors. Most of us do not mean to do this, but our busy schedules and our daily demands often set the stage for ignoring students when they are doing what we desire. If you will think about it for a moment, I believe you will agree that it is relatively easy to pay little attention to a youngster when he is doing just what we want. When the student is good, it gives us a chance to work with other students who need our help, or it gives us a chance to relax for a minute or two. Unfortunately, it is this lack of attention at the time the student is doing what we wish that gets many of us into trouble. Thinking about behavior pairs, however, can help us avoid many difficulties.

Since it is so easy to accidentally develop the habit of responding to less desired behaviors with the intention of reducing them, without also responding to more appropriate behaviors, let me present you with another key.

KEY:	If by your actions you attempt to reduce the occurrence of a disturbing behavior, a behavior that has been attended to or reinforced by you or the student's peers in the past, you *must* offer the student an alternatively more appropriate behavior. You cannot simply reduce a behavior without presenting the student with another one by which he can, once again, gain your attention and recognition.

EIGHTEENTH YOUDOIT

This is an extremely important exercise. I think you will be surprised at what you find.

Visit your observation school. Select a child (or two children) and count the number of times the teacher responds in a negative way to one of his less desired behaviors. Then count the number of times the teacher responds in a positive way to one of the student's behaviors that is incompatible to the one being "punished."

NINETEENTH YOUDOIT

If you found in the above youdoit that the teacher failed to respond positively to an alternatively more appropriate behavior, determine what that behavior could be. Develop a behavior pair and, if you have a good relationship with the teacher, offer it to him!

When a teacher responds in a negative way to only that which disturbs him he puts himself in a completely self-defeating position. First, the approach does *not* tell the student what to do. Thus he will have a difficult time knowing how to avoid future negative reactions. Second, the continued use of the negative approach may actually end up maintaining the very behavior the teacher wishes to reduce. The negative statements and actions may become forms of positive reinforcement for the student. That is another downhill cycle.

During the eighteenth youdoit, did you observe a teacher punish a student for being out of his seat? What did he do, then, when the student returned to his seat? If a youngster was scolded for not paying attention, was he also thanked for doing the opposite? If a student was embarrassed in front of his peers for offering an incorrect answer, was he also praised for an accurate answer?

If the youngster's more appropriate behavior did not result in some positive reaction from the teacher, then the teacher is on his way to being up the proverbial creek!

PUNISHMENT[4]

From Neil Postman and Charles Weingartner's, *The School Book:*

[4] We will be looking at punishment solely in terms of its application in schools. Some of the issue and points raised are more generic to classrooms than the research laboratory. For a more technical discussion regarding punishment, see N. H. Azrin, and W. C. Holz, "Punishment." In W. A. Honig (Editor), *Operant Behavior: Areas of Research and Application.* New York: Appleton-Century-Crofts, 1966.

"...the legal right of public school officials to inflict violent bodily punishment without being guilty of assault and battery is so well established in common law that many state codes do not even mention it. Moreover, at the present time, at least thirteen states explicity *do* mention it, and permit it (California, Delaware, Florida, Hawaii, Michigan, Montana, Nevada, North Carolina, Ohio, Pennsylvania, South Dakota, Vermont, and Virginia). There are several court actions pending whose purpose is to challenge the legality of corporal punishment. But it would appear that the courts will continue to uphold the practice."

"One of the more depressing features of the whole situation is that most school people favor corporal punishment: In a 1969 survey conducted by the National Education Association, 65 percent of the elementary school teachers polled, and 55 percent of the secondary teachers, said they favored 'judicious use' of violent bodily punishment. A comment made by the president of the Pittsburgh Teachers Federation tells an awful lot about where things are at. . . . 'Until somebody comes up with an alternative, we'll support it (corporal punishment). It's a quick way to show disapproval— like the city giving me a ticket when I park illegally.' " (p. 146)

The legal issue Postman and Weingartner speak of, although important, is only one side of the picture. The justification, or lack thereof, for physical punishment in our public schools must rest on what the research suggests about the long-range effects of punishment and *not* on a court decision regarding legality.

Legal or otherwise, few advocates for humane treatment of children would argue with a parent's decision to use physical punishment if the spanking prevented the child from playing in a busy street or experimenting with matches. Additionally, few would argue with the careful and limited use of punishment if that punishment reduced the occurrence of seriously self-destructive behavior manifested by an "autistic" child, thereby enabling the child to become more fully functioning and less incapacitated. But when we consider physical punishment in our schools, are we talking about those types of behaviors?

Suppose the courts find the issue of corporal punishment to be legal. What then? Presently, it is certainly legal for you, by *your* choice, to drink tea that has been laced with arsenic. It's just not very healthy to do so. To my knowledge, there is no law that prevents you from standing in the middle of a train track with the hopes of stopping the oncoming train with a flyswatter. If you suddenly find out that it is perfectly legal for your neighborhood plumber to remove your appendix, are you going to lie down and say, "Have at it?" The question of legality is not the central issue. More important is the question, "What does the 'judicious use' do to the school child?"

In my view, those advocates of corporal punishment for public school children who are waiting for a court decision have grown too old to remember what it is like to be on the receiving end! For the most part, they have also forgotten how they felt about the person who did the punishing.

A few years ago, one of the major television networks presented a "special" showing a teacher (from a private boys school in England) whipping his students *before* class to show them what *would* happen if they misbehaved in class. At the time of the viewing, I wondered what would happen to the teacher's future whipping behavior if, prior to his entering church, his minister beat the "daylights" out of him, thus showing what would happen if the teacher failed to pay attention to what the clergyman was about to say.

Regardless of what a court decides, it is imperative that you look carefully at what physical punishment does before you consider its use.

PUNISHMENT—MORE THAN ONE DEFINITION?

Most people agree that actions such as spankings, slaps, and the like are examples of physical punishment. This type of punishment is defined as the *application* of a physically punishing event given immediately after the occurrence of a particular behavior. (Remember, a spanking will only be a form of punishment if a youngster stops doing whatever it was that brought him the spanking.)

There are other actions that do not employ the application of a physically punishing event that are also generally referred to as types of punishment. These other actions are often considered more humane and are, therefore, separated from physical or corporal punishment. In reviewing these other measures, Dr. B. F. Skinner (1968) has written:

> "The brutality of corporal punishment and the viciousness it breeds in both teacher and student have. . .led to reform. Usually this has meant little more than shifting to noncorporal measures, of which education can boast an astonishing list. Ridicule (now largely verbalized, but once symbolized by the dunce cap or by forcing the

student to sit facing a wall), scolding, sarcasm, criticism, incarceration ('being kept after school'), extra school or home work, the withdrawal of privileges, forced labor, ostracism, being put on silence and fines—these are some of the devices which have permitted the teacher to spare the rod without spoiling the child. In some respects they are less objectionable than corporal punishment, but the pattern remains: the student spends a great part of his day doing things he does not want to do." (p. 96)

Whether scolding, sarcasm, ridicule, and the like are less objectionable than corporal punishment is a debatable issue. Like physical punishment, they most certainly work against the teacher. If you have ever observed the reactions of many students to severe sarcastic ridicule I think you will agree that such actions can be devastating. Students who are told that they are worthless, that they are dummies or stupid, may very well believe that the evaluations are correct because, as Stagner (1961) has pointed out, "the child. . .comes. . .to accept the image of himself, as reflected in the evaluations of those around him. . . . The child's self-image reflects the opinions others hold of him; he accepts their characterizations of him to no inconsiderable degree. . . ." (pp. 185-186)

Furthermore, teachers who consistently ridicule a particular student may well set that student up *against* his peers and, as any student knows, being an "outsider" can be much more painful than a spanking. Sulzer and Mayer (1972) note that, ". . . peer reactions may pose a serious problem particularly to the well-being of the punished student," when that student is singled out and reprimanded sarcastically.

An obvious question at this point asks, "Is there a way a teacher can reduce the occurrence of disturbing, annoying, and disruptive behaviors without having to resort to corporal punishment, ridicule, and sarcasm?" The answer is yes, and we will look at that now. (For your information, many professionals and parents do not consider the following alternatives to be forms of punishment in the strict sense of the word. Whether they are right or not is not critical. What is important, however, is that these alternative means for reducing behavior do not produce the same type of side-effects (Bandura, 1969) often seen with corporal punishment.

THE REMOVAL OR WITHHOLDING OF POSITIVE REINFORCEMENT

Let us look quickly at what can happen when we apply punishment (spankings, paddlings, sarcastic verbal reprimands). I think you will then see why an alternative approach should be used if the occasion arises where you need to reduce the occurrence of an undesired behavior.

1. *Associative Effects.* When a student experiences physical punishment in a classroom, all that is present in that class—teacher, course work, "school"—will begin to become what are called conditioned punishers. People and places will acquire some of the properties of punishment merely by their association with punishment.

2. *Avoidance Effects.* You and I will work very hard to *avoid* that which we perceive as threatening or punishing, be the object of our avoidance primary (a hot stove) or conditioned (teacher). " . . .the child who is punished excessively learns to avoid not only the spankings. . .but the people who did the punishing and the places where it occurred. . ." (Becker et al. 1971, p. 155). Physical punishment sets the stage for any behavior that enables the student to avoid punishment. In schools, which can become conditioned punishers through association, one of the most effective ways of avoiding continued punishment is to avoid school—either physically or mentally.

3. *Feelings Effects.* Classrooms that are enjoyable are, by definition, fun places to be. Classrooms that are punishing are best avoided. Physical punishment often elicits fear and anxiety. Neither feeling is compatible with a fun classroom. "Because punishment elicits anger, frustration, and counteraggression, places where punishment is used are miserable places in which to live. People who resort to the excessive use of punishment become tense and uncomfortable themselves, provoke all manner of noncooperation in their circle of influence, and cause these people to be tense, too." (Ackerman, 1972, p. 19)

4. *Generalization Effects.* The behavior that is physically punished is not the only behavior that will begin to decrease. Other behaviors, many of which are essential for learning, will also begin to decrease.

5. *Counteraggression Effects.* One way to react to highly punishing and aggressive people is through counteraggression. Schools and teachers who use considerable punishment to deal with their

students are setting themselves to be "hit" back. "During the 1967-68 school year New York City spent 1.21 million dollars to replace broken windows. In the same year, the city of Chicago put a price tag of nearly 2 million dollars on school vandalism. . . .

Some observers have told us that it is the reaction of the young against the establishment and against authority. If that is the case, why don't we hear about the broken windows of other establishment buildings such as churches, factories, car dealers, hospitals, city halls, and libraries?" (Bushell, 1973, pp. 73-74) It's an interesting question, isn't it?

Any or all of these effects will ultimately work against the teacher and the student. Neither will feel comfortable, and both will try to avoid one another—that has to be directly opposite of what a good teacher wants to happen in his or her classroom. I think most teachers would agree that we are better off if students want to be with us instead of wanting to avoid us; that we will accomplish more when students feel comfortable and happy instead of angry and frustrated; and that the school itself will work better when students work for us instead of aggressing against us. Although no cure-all, using the withdrawal of positive reinforcement in place of physical punishment to teach students what not to do will help us avoid the above mentioned effects, while also helping us to set the kind of atmosphere that is more conducive to exciting learning.

A Critical Advantage of Removing Positive Reinforcement

There is another point regarding the removal of positive reinforcement that, perhaps, has occurred to you. Inherent in the loss of reinforcement is the opportunity to earn it back. A teacher, therefore, can influence both sides of her behavior pairs by removing the reinforcer when an undesired behavior has occurred and reestablishing it when an alternatively more appropriate behavior has been observed. If the teacher is reasonably consistent the student will learn that his behavior results in fairly predictable outcomes. He will see that his behavior has purpose, that it is meaningful. In a short while, he will be able to say to himself, "When I do this, such and such happens." He learns that he has a choice. He also learns what will usually happen as a result of his choice.

In a very true sense, the student learns that he basically controls his own reinforcers.

It's the Students' Choice

Mr. Wallin had spent many hours coming up with a plan for his eighth-grade science class. He had developed a test that was administered to each student in class. The test was used to estimate each student's present performance level. Based on the information obtained from the test, the class was divided into groups of four or five students. Each group had a leader (a student who had performed well on the test) who was responsible for helping the other students in his group. The remainder of the group was composed of students who had performed at different levels of proficiency on the test. Mr. Wallin had used this small group approach many times, finding that the students seemed more likely to discuss their deficiencies with their peers.

The groups were all given the same daily project, which related to the day's or week's topic. Mr. Wallin would give a brief presentation to the entire class, explaining certain ideas regarding the project, and then he would divide his class into their groups. Each member of the group was given the responsibility for solving a component of the class project. The components would then be synthesized until the group developed the final solution to the presented problem. After checking the group's answer, the team leader would present the intact project to the teacher. If the answer was accurate and complete, the students (in that group) were allowed to spend whatever remaining time there was at the activity center (the library or in back of Mr. Wallin's classroom). Mr. Wallin had been teaching for several years. During these years, he had tried various approaches to bring about a good, positive working atmosphere for his students. He had grown weary of his occasional use of threats, finding that they rarely worked in the long run, while also finding that the threats and punishment drained him of his own enthusiasm. He had also grown tired of his self-appointed position of "behavior monitor."

Prior to the initiation of his latest approach, Mr. Wallin held a meeting with his entire class. The purpose of the meeting was to discuss which behaviors would be considered appropriate for his classroom as well as the behaviors deemed acceptable for the time spent in the activity centers. He pointed out to his class that it would be necessary for each student to help his peers to arrive at the solution to the group's assigned problem. He mentioned that when the students were enjoying the free-time period in the activity center, they would have to remain relatively quiet. With this introduction, he turned the discussion over to the class, asking them for help in developing classroom/activity center guidelines for behavior. Once the rules were established, the students, along with Mr. Wallin, came to an agreement about the consequences of the accepted behavior pairs. The decision was simple. If the guidelines were followed the students were permitted to remain at the center for the total available time. If the guidelines were not followed the misbehaving student would lose the activity center privilege for the remainder of the period. The class understood and agreed to the fact that staying and enjoying the activity center was entirely up to them. They would moinitor their own behavior.

The agreed-on guidelines were strictly followed. During the first days, a few students "tested out" the rules and, as a result, lost the center's privilege for that day. On several occasions, Mr. Wallin had to mediate some problems, primarily dealing with suggested "exceptions" to the rules. When appropriate, the exceptions were presented to the class for a decision.

The system worked well. Mr. Wallin allowed his students to govern their own behavior as established by the class' guidelines. Based on the teacher's observations of his class' behavior, the students appeared to appreciate their teacher's approach.

A General Word of Caution

Your behavior and mine is greatly influenced by the results of our reactions to our students. This means that when we do something that results in a desired outcome from our students, *we* are being reinforced and *we* will probably repeat our actions in the future. Suppose, for example, that we have observed one of our young students continually pushing another student out of the way in order to take the supplies the second student has been enjoying. For most teachers, this will be an example of an undesired behavior. Suppose further that instead of scolding the child or perhaps repeating your previous statement that it is not nice to do such things, you inform the youngster that as a result of his behavior, he will have to sit quietly in his seat for a few moments without any supplies. Instead of sitting quietly, he protests your actions. Let's say he cries and whines. Since this behavior is occurring in class, there is a good chance that it will be disturbing to the other youngsters which, in turn, will make it additionally disturbing to you.

As a result, you will be placed under a certain amount of pressure to put a halt to the whining and crying. You may find, quite accidentally, that by returning the supplies to the youngster his crying ceases. Since relative calm has returned to the classroom, *your* behavior of returning the supplies has been reinforced. Unfortunately, your behavior has also reinforced the youngster's whining and crying. I think you can see that *two* behaviors will likely begin to increase, the whining and the returning of the supplies. Obviously, the two behaviors will work against one another. The next time the student cries *you* will be more inclined to return the material which, in turn, will increase *his* future whining (and pushing).

It is very important to remember, that *whatever behavior* is immediately followed by the *return* of a desired reinforcer will tend to occur again. Therefore, when you return the reinforcer, watch carefully what behavior is occurring prior to the return.

TWENTIETH YOUDOIT

Look once again at the above pushing example (p. 124). Assume that you are interested in helping the student learn to be more cooperative, to share the supplies instead of pushing.

Question:

1. Do you consider the teacher's reaction to the child's pushing compatible with teaching him to work cooperatively?

   a. _____

   _____

   _____

   _____

   _____

2. How could you use the return of a reinforcer, specifically the object

that was obtained by pushing, to accomplish the goal of cooperative sharing?

a. _____

_____

_____

_____

_____

_____

_____

3. Once sharing was observed, what would you do?

a. _____

_____

THREE APPROACHES USING THE WITHDRAWAL OF POSITIVE REINFORCEMENT

Before deciding which of the following procedures for reducing behavior will be most helpful to you and your students, there are several factors that you need to consider. Think about them carefully, because the incorrect use of the following procedures will create problems that are best avoided.

Type of Behavior You Are Observing

You have had the opportunity to observe several teachers and their reactions to many different types of student behaviors. You probably did not agree with the way the teachers dealt with some of the observed behaviors. One of the problems we have is that we do not all feel the same about the degree of severity of the behaviors. For some, a particular behavior is viewed as highly disturbing—even destructive to the class atmosphere. For others, the same behavior is perhaps annoying and bothersome, but nothing more. (To complicate matters, our perceptions about the severity of the behavior may well change, depending on our present mood, time of day, one student demonstrating the behavior instead of another, and what we had for dinner the previous evening.)

In many cases, our reaction to a behavior is based on our feelings regarding this degree of severity. One of the first steps, then, for you to take when selecting an approach is to give careful consideration to the importance of the behavior you are observing. In your view, is the behavior annoying and bothersome, but not disruptive to the class? Is it more than annoying? Is it physically dangerous to the youngster as well as his peers? Is the behavior serious enough to require that it be stopped immediately or can it, perhaps, be allowed to run its course?

Where the Behavior Occurs

Selection of an approach is somewhat dependent on where the "misbehavior" is occuring. In most cases, it will be much easier for you to deal with a behavior when it occurs in your presence alone instead of in the presence of you and thirty other students. That is quite obvious. A second set of questions for you to consider, therefore, deals with this factor of location. Does the behavior most often involve just you and the student? Or does the behavior occur smack in the middle of the entire classroom where "everybody" becomes involved? (Notice that the behavior factor and the location factor often have to be considered together. A normally disruptive behavior loses a good deal of its severity if it occurs when you and the student are alone. On the other hand, a mildly annoying behavior can be likened to a tornado if it occurs in a less favorable location.)

Reactions of Other Students to the Behavior

Behaviors that are attended to and reinforced by peers are more difficult to deal with than behaviors that are occuring mainly as a result of teacher attention. The numbers of "outside" influencers are of particular importance. The decision regarding your approach should be reached only after you make an earnest effort to determine who is basically maintaining the student's "misbehavior."

THE WITHDRAWAL OF SOCIAL REINFORCEMENT

Sometimes, no response is the best response you can make to certain types of behaviors. In this case, no response means withholding *all* attention and recognition (including warnings, reminders, and glances toward the student) for the *total duration* of the undesired behavior. If the necessary factors are present, the ignoring of a behavior can be a very effective approach to reduce a behavior. Let's look at some of the necessary factors.

1. *Behavior.* Behaviors that can be ignored are those that are not physically dangerous to the student or his peers. Ignorable behaviors are also those that are annoying and disturbing, but not completely disruptive to the class. Being out of one's seat; calling out an answer when hand raising has been requested; making "funny" noises; and the like, are behaviors that are best ignored. "Attention-getting" behaviors would be a general classification of ignorable responses.

2. *Location.* Any location where the inappropriate behavior can be allowed to run its course without appreciably disturbing others is an acceptable place for ignoring the response. For example, a loud verbal protest can be more easily ignored on the playground than in the library. Likewise, a tantrum is less disruptive when it occurs in the presence of only the teacher than in the presence of the classroom during a quiet discussion period. This does not mean that the tantrum cannot be ignored in the classroom. If it does not disrupt the teacher-student activity, then the classroom is just as appropriate as any place. In other words, any location is fine, as long as it does not disrupt the ongoing activity.

3. *Student Reaction.* If a behavior is being attended to by the teacher *and* the youngster's peers, *both* sources of attention must be withheld before the behavior will be significantly reduced. If the teacher is unable to elicit the cooperation of the other students, his own ignoring of the behavior will be only minimally helpful. For this factor, the teacher's relationship with the entire class becomes the central issue. If he has a good, cooperative relationship, he will be in a better position to ask for and receive the other students' help. The students will be more inclined to work *for* him, instead of *against* him. Most important, the teacher's demonstrated approval and appreciation will be more reinforcing to the other students than the reinforcement they are experiencing from the one disruptive student. As coarse as it may sound, we are talking about competition. Before a teacher can even get into the game, he must be viewed as positive, pleasant, understanding, and a "good Joe." If

he is not viewed this way, he will not be able to reduce behaviors through the use of withholding social reinforcement since, in the eyes of his students, he *will have none* to withhold!

4. *Behavior Pairs.* Before this approach will have any long-lasting effects, the teacher must determine an alternatively more appropriate behavior that will take the place of the inappropriate behavior. If possible the two behaviors should be incompatible. As soon as the more desired response is observed, the teacher must immediately reinforce the desired alternative. If the teacher decides to ignore the student who calls out an answer by not recognizing his response, then he must also respond to him positively when he raises his hand to be recognized. This will help the student understand what to do as well as what not to do.

5. *Caution.* If a behavior has, in the past, brought a youngster attention and recognition, he is not about to let go of it simply because the teacher has decided to no longer respond to the behavior. What often happens is that the behavior will temporarily increase—sort of a one last ditch effort—before it begins to decrease. It is essential that the behavior be totally ignored throughout this period of increase. Otherwise, the behavior will be that much more difficult to reduce. Be prepared, therefore, for this increase so you won't accidentally respond to it in *any way*. If, for various reasons, the increase does not occur, don't complain!

Resting a Foot Rester

Mrs. Tory was not even aware of the problem until a colleague asked her if one of her students was putting water and mud on a chair in the classroom. Apparently, a student from the following class had sat in a "sea" of mud and was quite upset about it. "I don't know, but I will check. I think the seat is vacant during my period," Mrs. Tory told her friend.

On the following day, Mrs. Tory watched the chair in question. As she thought, no one sat there. However, toward the end of the period, she discovered the culprit. Perhaps without realizing it, Eddie, who was sitting right behind the chair, nonchanlantly placed his feet on the seat and, within a second or two, they had left their mark. Without much thought, Mrs. Tory walked briskly to where Eddie was sitting. In an abrupt manner, she scolded Eddie and "requested" that he go to the washroom to clean off his shoes and to bring back a wet paper towel so he could clean off the seat. Somewhat shaken, Eddie did as requested. Although there were a few giggles, for the most part, Eddie's exit, entrance, and cleaning job received little attention from his classmates. Eddie apologized, as did the teacher for her abruptness.

Two days later, Mrs. Tory noticed that one of the students in the back of the room began to prop his feet on a display table close to his seat. Unlike Eddie, this second student, Charlie, was not one of Mrs. Tory's better students. She had had some minor problems with him before. Not wanting to create a scene, Mrs. Tory quietly walked back to Charlie and politely asked him to place his feet on the floor, which he did. Some ten minutes later, the youngster's feet were again found resting on the table. Mrs. Tory went back to him and, in a slightly more harsh tone, reminded him of her initial request. When he returned his feet to the floor, Mrs. Tory turned and walked to the front of the room. She was quite perturbed by the student's actions, feeling that he was being purposely disruptive. For the remainder of the class period she did not take her eyes off the student, and he kept his feet on the floor.

By the end of the week, Mrs. Tory and Charlie had three additional confrontations regarding his foot-resting behavior. She was bound and determined to stop his antics "even if it takes telling him not to each time he does it." By Wednesday of the next week, she had had it and she told Charlie "in no uncertain terms" that the next time he placed his feet anyplace other than the floor he would find himself sitting across from the vice principal. That afternoon, he was there.

TWENTY-FIRST YOUDOIT

I want you to assume the role of the teacher. Think about the three basic factors (behavior, location, and student reaction) we have just discussed. I am going to ask you to come up with an idea to deal with Charlie's foot resting. First, however, I would like to ask you a few questions.

1. How would you classify the target behavior (footresting) in regards to the issue of severity?

    a. Physically dangerous.
    b. Annoying.
    c. Disruptive.

d. Other_____.

(When you have finished compare your answer with some of your classmates. If there are differences take a few moments in class to discuss the rationale for your choice.)

2. Is the location, as described, suitable for using the withdrawal of social reinforcement?

        yes   no

a. How did you arrive at your answer?

_____

_____

_____

_____

3. If someone were to ask you if Mrs. Tory's reactions were reinforcing to Charlie, what would be your answer? What evidence would you offer in support of your answer?

_____

_____

_____

_____

_____

_____

Please fill in the following chart. I would like you to consider strongly the use of withdrawing social reinforcement as a means to reduce the occurrence of Charlie's target behavior. (If you have a compelling reason to try something else, ask your professor for time to explain the reason for your view.)

Teacher's Initial Program

Behavior	Environment's Reaction	Results
Desired	Teacher's reaction—	
Undesired	Teacher's reaction—	

Your New Program

Behavior	Environment's Reaction
Desired	Your reaction—
Undesired	Your reaction—
Resting feet on display table	

How did you do? Did you discover immediately that you needed to develop a behavior pair? If so, great. If not, keep that in mind. Without a behavior pair, Charlie is going to find his own way to gain your attention, and it may be placing his entire body on the display table.

From the information I gave you, it certainly appears that Mrs. Tory's attention was very reinforcing to the student. Did you alter when it was given? If so, that is also great. If not, remember that in order to help Charlie learn what is expected of him, reinforcement immediately after the desired alternative response (and it did occur!) would be very helpful.

The situation I presented was pretty "ideal." Charlie wasn't hurting anyone, and it is unlikely that he could have hurt himself. (An orthopedic surgeon might not agree.) The rest of the youngsters paid little or no attention to him, so his behavior was not particularly disruptive to the class. (Unfortunately, Mrs. Tory might not agree.) The behavior occurred in relative isolation—the "problem" was really only between Mrs. Tory and Charlie—so the teacher, if she choose, could have let the behavior run its course without creating any problem for the rest of the class. But realistically, not all of the problem situations teachers face are as simple as the one just described. Therefore, let us change our story somewhat. We will "push" Charlie and the rest of the class a little bit, while we look at the second approach that withdraws something besides social reinforcement.

THE WITHDRAWAL OF MATERIAL REINFORCEMENT

When we speak of withholding or withdrawing material reinforcers in a school setting, we are usually referring to the loss of supplies, when they are abused; the loss of a percentage of time spent at an enjoyable activity; or missing out entirely on a movie, field trip, or classroom game. In fact, the loss of any activity included in the previously mentioned reinforcement menu could be used with this second approach.

As with the approach of withholding attention and recognition, this second idea enables the teacher to avoid the use of scolding, reprimanding, and sarcasm. Instead, the teacher matter of factly removes access to a desired activity as soon as an inappropriate behavior has been observed. Given the fact that we would like to use this approach as infrequently as possible (thereby maintaining its effectiveness), it is advisable to determine *and* discuss with the entire class what we actually mean by "inappropriate." Ideally, prior to any infraction, the students should know which behaviors are to be *avoided,* which behaviors are deemed *acceptable,* and what will happen as a *result* of both. This discussion decreases the mystery and ambiguity often found in the classroom, and it increases the chances that the youngsters will know what is expected of them. (As previously mentioned, whenever possible, the students should have the opportunity to voice their opinions regarding the establishment of the behavior pairs.) Once again, let's look at our factors and see how they relate to this second approach.

1. *Behavior.*   Just about any behavior can effectively be dealt with by using this second approach. Even behaviors that are potentially dangerous can be dramatically influenced. For example, a youngster who flings his bat on the playground loses a portion of his play time, while a student who is observed horseplaying in a stairway may have to forfeit access to a movie or other class activity. Behaviors that are less severe can also be handled by the loss of some material reinforcement. Excessive noise, talking with a neighbor, throwing paper, and failure to do any work are a few examples. By and large, behaviors that cannot be effectively ignored either because of location, peer influence, teacher disposition, and the like can be reduced by having the youngster give up something he would like to have.

2. *Location.*   One of the prime advantages for this approach is that location is not a critical issue. It can be used within or outside the classroom with relative ease. Keep in mind, however, that its excessive use will result in a weakening of its effectiveness.

3. *Student Reaction.*   Peer reaction is an important factor only if the misbehaving student views his friends' reactions as more meaningful than the loss of the material reinforcement. If that is the case, then the teacher will have to determine a way to nullify the peer reinforcement, usually with the loss of reinforcement for the *participators* (and not *all* the other students, unless they all are participating). Notice that this is similar to the problem mentioned with the withdrawal of social reinforcement—competition. Most teachers are able to find a material reinforcer potent enough to influence the few students who reinforce the initially misbehaving youngster.

4. *Behavior Pairs.*   Most critical is the idea of providing the student with a means to earn back the removed reinforcer. A youngster must know which of his behaviors will result in the return of the

reinforcer as well as what he must do to prevent its future loss. A clear specification of the agreed on behavior pair is usually all that is necessary. *When* to return the reinforcer is, however, a delicate matter. The easiest statement I can make is that the reinforcer is returned as soon as the youngster begins to behave appropriately. Unfortunately, the matter is not that simple.

Suppose that a student misuses the classroom's record player; he scratches the records and is very rough with the needle. In order to deal with this, the teacher notifies the student that he will not be able to use the record player for several minutes as a consequence of his inconsiderate behavior. The youngster is asked to sit in his seat, which he does with no protesting. After several minutes of quiet behavior, he is offered the opportunity to return to the record player. Technically, his quiet sitting has been reinforced. We have yet to be able to reinforce appropriate use of the record player.

In most cases, the teacher will ask the student if he is ready to play "nicely." Assuming the student's answer is yes, we are now put in a position of relying on the youngster's assurance instead of his behavior. As you well know, assurance and actual behavior do not always go hand in hand. Therefore, two things are very important. First, if the youngster "keeps his word" and plays with the record player in a manner that is viewed as acceptable, then it is imperative that the teacher positively attend to the more desired activity, since this will be the first chance to act on the correct behavior. Second, in the event that the youngster does not carry through with his assurance, he must once again lose access to the activity, but for a longer period of time. This amount of time is a difficult thing to determine. It should be sufficient to deter further misbehaving. Ultimately, the youngster's behavior is the best barometer, once again. Because of the importance of this issue, I will offer you an example I presented in an earlier book written for parents (Macht, 1975).

Robert's Flying Bat

In his enthusiasm to learn to hit a ball, Robert would fling his plastic bat about twenty feet when he would strike out. His father was a student of the game, having played it for his college team. He wanted to help his son learn to hit the ball but, more important, he wanted him to learn to control his temper and no longer throw his bat when he would strike out.

Most of Robert's practice sessions took place in his backyard. His father would serve as pitcher, his mother would play both infield and outfield, and his younger sister would usually just get in the way. Each of the family would take turns hitting the ball, although Robert ended up having about three times more batting practice than the rest of the family combined.

Robert was told that the next time the bat was thrown he would have to sit on the sidelines until he was ready to practice and no longer throw his bat. He was told that it is certainly okay to be upset when striking out, but he could no longer throw the bat. Robert agreed, and everything went well for the next two times he struck out. He was warmly praised for being a good sport. However, on his following turn, the bat went flying. Father immediately placed Robert in a chair on the patio, reminding him that he would not be able to play for a little while since he threw the bat.

Robert was upset and he exclaimed that he didn't want to play anyway. He sat on the chair while his sister took her turn. After about five minutes Robert asked his father if he could have another turn. "Only if you promise not to throw the bat," was Father's reply. The very next time Robert failed to hit the ball, the bat was thrown. As if to indicate that he knew he had done something wrong, he immediately apologized and promised not to do it again. Father, however, sent him to his chair, telling Robert that although he appreciated his apology he nevertheless did throw the bat and he would have to sit out for fifteen minutes. Robert put up quite a fuss, but he drew little attention from his family. After the fifteen-minute period, Robert returned to the game. Although he still was upset when he failed to connect with the ball, the bat throwing had ceased.

Cautions.

First, carefully watch the behavior that earns the reinforcer back. Make certain that it is one you would like the student to repeat in the near future. Second (*please* think about this), the withdrawal of material reinforcement is extremely easy to use. It is so easy that you may find yourself relying on it. Don't fall into the trap of reflexively pulling a desired activity away from a student anytime he does something you find objectionable. Before you act, consider whether your withholding of social reinforcement might be just as effective. Also, look at your own behavior. Are you accidentally reinforcing the response that is ultimately causing the student to lose his activity? Could you reinforce another response, thereby enabling the student to avoid the loss of the reinforcer entirely?

Charlie and His Friends—A Little More Mischievous

When Charlie returned from the vice-principal's office, he made it perfectly clear to his close friends that the experience wasn't all that bad. In fact, since it enabled him to miss a good portion of the math class, it was well worth it. He quietly suggested to his comrades that they, too, try it. "Maybe the old lady will send us all down to Mr. Farnum's office."

Having the "bug" placed in the ears was all that was necessary. Within a very short period of time one of the other youngsters, sitting in the back of the room, placed his feet on the display table. Mrs. Tory immediately saw this happen, but decided to pay no attention to what was going on. Seeing that nothing happened, a third did the same, only he used the back of an occupied chair for his ottoman. Before Mrs. Tory had completed her explanation of an algebraic equation, five pairs of feet could be found resting on something other than the floor.

"It seems as though we have a little game going," Mrs. Tory began as she put the chalk down and walked to the back of the class. "I believe we had better end it now. Charlie, you will go back to Mr. Farnum's office immediately and you will stay there the rest of the period."

"Yes, ma'am," Charlie replied, with a smile, as he looked toward his friends.

"Billy, you and Dave, Harry, and Mike will stay with me during the next period. Since you are obviously tired, having to rest you feet, I don't think it is fair to ask you to have recess. You can rest with me."

"But. . . ," Charlie began and then quickly stopped. As he left the room he noticed that Dave, Harry, and Mike were not smiling.

On the following day, Dave, Harry, and Mike, despite the urging from Charlie, kept their feet on the floor. "Come on, man, we don't want to miss recess again," they said in unison.

"Hey, I don't care about that dumb recess. Basketball is no fun anyway," Billy quickly added, and up went his feet.

"I guess you haven't learned your lesson. Charlie, you may leave—Billy you will again miss recess," Mrs. Tory informed the two youngsters.

Mrs. Tory was a little concerned. Over the next few days, both boys continued their antics, even though Charlie was consistently sent to the vice-principal's office and Billy continued to miss recess.

TWENTY-SECOND YOUDOIT

Let's see if you can help Mrs. Tory with Billy. We won't worry about Charlie for now.

Question:

1. Was the teacher's approach used with Dave, Harry, and Mike successful?

              yes   no

  a. How do you know that your answer is correct?

_____

_____

_____

_____

2. Was the teacher's approach used with Billy successful?

              yes   no

  a. How do you know that your answer is correct?

_____

_____

_____

_____

If your answer to number 2 was yes, reread the scenario. If your answer was no, then before you read any further, take a few moments to develop an idea for Mrs. Tory that might be of some help.

On the following day, during Billy's imposed "rest" period, he approached Mrs. Troy while she was grading some papers.

"I know I have to stay for another twenty minutes," he began, "but I wonder if you would let me leave a few minutes early?"

"Why, Billy?" Mrs. Tory asked.

"Well, we are having a special. . .a special band practice for the school picnic, you know, the one next week. I really would like to go practice."

"Do you think I should let you go?" the teacher asked.

"Well," Billy paused for a moment, "I guess not."

"Why don't you sit down for a few minutes," Mrs. Tory said, "and I will think about it." Billy sat down as requested and Mrs. Tory watched him from the corner of her eye. She noticed that he kept looking at the clock.

"Billy, come here for a moment. You'd like to go practice, wouldn't you?"

"Yes."

"Do you know what I would like?"

"I think you would like me to keep my feet off the table, right?"

"How about on the floor?" she added. "Okay, my young friend. We have an agreement, don't we?"

"You bet."

"Have a good time at your practice. I'll see how you do tomorrow in class."

"Thanks, Mrs. Tory. Thanks very much," he warmly replied as he departed.

The next morning, Charlie made his "pitch," only to be told, "Forget it, Charlie. She was pretty good to me. We have an agreement and I don't feel like missing band practice."

Of course, there was no way for you to know that Billy was concert master for the school band. You probably did not incorporate it into your suggested program for Mrs. Tory. But if you recognized that the loss of recess simply was not meaningful to Billy and you suggested that the teacher would have to find something else with which to influence Billy, then your idea was probably fine.

It is unlikely that the teacher could have continued to ignore all the students involved in the foot game. There is a good chance they would have reinforced each other sufficiently to maintain their antics. With the exception of Charlie, Mrs. Tory's alternative approach was quite successful.

Before moving on, there are two points that deserve mentioning. First, Mrs. Tory was able to be reasonably calm about the entire matter. She didn't have to raise her voice or continually threaten the students. Instead, she matter of factly used the loss of a desired reinforcer to bring to an end what in her view was a disturbing behavior. Second, she kept her eyes and ears opened. She discovered what was meaningful to Billy by watching and listening to him. *He* told her what was reinforcing to him. When he was told that he would have to lose what he wanted, the game quickly ended.

Back to Charlie in a moment.

THE WITHDRAWAL OF ALL REINFORCEMENT

Unfortunately, there are times when neither the loss of social reinforcement nor the loss of a single material reinforcer will be sufficient to bring a severely disruptive behavior to an abrupt halt. On the other hand, the instances of severely disruptive behavior should be infrequent. If they are dealt with immediately they can become almost nonexistent.

This final approach involves removing the student from as many sources of reinforcement as possible. He literally is isolated for a brief period of time as soon as he demonstrates the severely inappropriate behavior. After the time period has ended, he is returned to the classroom or location where the incident took place.

This, too, is a *deceptively* easy procedure to use. Sending a youngster from the classroom, having him go to the principal's office, requiring that he sit in a seat in the nearby hallway or back of the classroom, or even sending him home, for the most part, requires little planning, thought or energy. It's simple! At the same time, be aware that this approach is one of the most difficult ones to use effectively. I assure you that teachers who have successfully used this approach in the past have spent a good deal of energy--thinking and planning.

Since this approach requires that a student be taken from one location and placed in a second location, the teacher is faced with the task of making certain that the *two* locations have very specific characteristics. To help you see what these necessary characteristics are, I will break the two locations down as follows.

Room (Location) Where the Student Is Taken FROM	Room (Location) Where the Student is Taken TO
1. This location must be very reinforcing for the student. He must want to be there and he must be willing to work hard to stay there. (This place, hopefully, is the student's classroom.)	1. This location must be as free of positive reinforcement, both material and social, as possible. The student must *not* want to be there. He must be willing to work hard to avoid being sent to this location.
2. This location must provide the student with positive reinforcement for appropriate behaviors—particularly	2. This location must *not* provide the student with any positive reinforcement for the misbehavior that was

Room (Location) Where the Student Is Taken FROM	Room (Location) Where the Student is Taken TO
for the behaviors that are incompatible with the misbehavior that is responsible for the student being sent from the room.	responsible for him being here, or any other inappropriate response. 3. The student must *not* be able to leave this location until either the expiration of the determined time period, or until he is given permission to leave by the teacher who sent him there in the first place.

That Place Is No Fun

Mr. Barber's second-grade class was an exciting learning center. The pupils were constantly being Introduced to new ideas and materials, and their enthusiasm indicted that they enjoyed what they were doing. One of the problems Mr. Barber had was the limited number of supplies available for his pupils. Because of this, the children had to continually take turns with what was available and, for the most part, the sharing was accomplished with little difficulty. Sandy, however, often made things unpleasant for some of her classmates. On the one hand, she would refuse to give up her materials when asked and, on the other hand, she would often just walk by someone who was working and grab away what was being used. Mr. Barber was usually able to convince Sandy to relinquish her supplies when the time came to do so, but he was not able to put a stop to her grabbing. He realized that the youngster was not being malicious, but she was also not being very considerate. Since he knew that the possibility of obtaining additional supplies was slight, he decided to talk with Sandy in the hope of reducing the grabbing incidents. He explained to her that if she grabbed again she would have to leave the study area and sit quietly in the back of the room for several minutes. He showed her the area that he had marked off with two bookcases and a portable, full-length blackboard. He also showed her the small chair that was surrounded by the cases and the chalkboard. He urged her not to grab anymore; if she wanted something, she was to come to him and he would see what could be done.

His explanation, however, was not heeded. Shortly after their conversation, Sandy not only grabbed some supplies, but she knocked a youngster over in the process. Without saying another word to her, he calmly took her by the hand and placed her in the chair in the marked-off area. He then told her that she would have to sit quietly for a few minutes, after which he would come and get her.

After three minutes of quiet behavior, Mr. Barber went to the back of the room. He told Sandy that if she wanted, she could return to the group, which she did. She sat down at a large table with several of her classmates and began working on some of the available material. Quickly, Mr. Barber walked over to her and quietly praised her for her behavior. She worked well for the remainder of the day.

Early the following day, she again was observed grabbing. She was immediately taken to the isolated area. After several minutes she was returned to the class. Her grabbing rarely occurred after that.

Mr. Barber's approach worked quickly. There was no screaming, yelling, threatening, or punishment. Based on Sandy's behavior, the marked-off area was not a fun place to be, because her grabbing decreased markedly. Regarding the factor of location, the place where Sandy was sent *from* was much more reinforcing than the place where she was sent *to*. Had it been the other way around, it is unlikely that the grabbing would have diminished.

Can't I Go Back to the First Place

It was flying paper clip time, at least for Larry. Despite repeated warnings, Larry would take an opened paper clip and a rubber band and, with considerable accuracy, send the clip flying most anyplace around the classroom. On this particular day, he missed the bulletin board and hit one of his classmates on the shoulder. After soothing the classmate, the teacher marched Larry down to the school's conference room and told him to stay there for fifteen minutes, then to return to class.

Although the teacher had not watched the clock, she was certain that Larry had been gone for more than the specified time. As she began to excuse herself from the classroom, Larry walked in and quietly sat in his chair. Before five minutes had passed, a loud clang was heard as a clip bounced off a metal wastebasket. Without hesitation, Larry was once again told to go to the conference room and to stay there for the remainder of the period.

Before the week was over, Larry was made to sit in the conference room several more times. Describing Larry as "incorrigible" to the school psychologist, the teacher asked her for some assistance.

"Let me know the next time you send him from the room," the psychologist told the teacher.

Almost immediately, the psychologist was told. She waited for a few moments and then, unannounced, she walked in on Larry, who was sitting in the conference room.

Larry was sitting very close to a large bay window. The curtains were drawn, opening an entire view of what was going on outside the school building. There were several men working close to the window, constructing an addition to the school's facilities. On occasion, one of the men would come close to the bay window and "touch" Larry's nose, which was pressed against the glass.

The psychologist quietly left the room and informed the teacher of what she had observed. She then went to the nurses's station to see if it was being used. The station was actually two rooms—one for resting and one for observation. The nurse indicated that the resting room was not occupied.

To describe this room as "gloomy" would be understating the case. There were no windows. There was a single bulb attached to a pre-Civil War fixture. There was one small wooden chair. And there was a "bed" that was actually a long cushion draped with paper that would impale you with a splinter if you ran your fingers across it.

The psychologist returned to the conference room. She and Larry walked from the room as one of the construction workers waved good-bye. Larry was told to sit in the small wooden chair in the nurse's station until someone came for him. Thereafter, the rubber band and paper clips were used as they were meant to be used.

Several factors, other than location, need to be considered before using this approach. First, our conversation. In many instances, we find ourselves talking with a youngster immediately after he has misbehaved. We ask him why he did it; we remind him not to do it again or, we warn him of the possible consequences if he does it again. Although rare, sometimes our little conversation is all that is necessary, since the youngster's misbehavior does not occur again. Most of the times, however, we are not so fortunate. We find that even with our conversation, the misbehavior is repeated several times. As you now know, our conversation is usually very reinforcing to students and, as a result, our questions, reminders, and warnings may be partially maintaining the very behavior we wish to decrease. This possibility is particularly important now. We do not want to use this final approach any more than is absolutely necessary. We must, therefore, guard against the accidental reinforcement of the very behavior responsible for the isolation of the student. To do this, we need to limit the amount of conversation with the student *immediately after* he misbehaves. Without fanfare, scolding, pleading, reminding, and explaining, we remove the student from the classroom and calmly take him to the isolation area. We might say, "You cannot stay here and fight," but that is all. Our explanations and reminders of what will happen as a result of misbehavior should come well before any misbehavior or well after the misbehavior has taken place *while* the youngster is working *appropriately*. "I am very pleased that you are working so nicely. I much prefer that you do this than fight, so you can stay with us instead of having to sit in the isolation area," is the only type of explanation or comment that should be necessary.

Second (perhaps this is only relevant for the younger student), it is important that the child be removed from the isolation area only after a few minutes of quiet behavior. He should *not* be returned to the classroom while he is loudly protesting. Remember, behavior is always being influenced by the environment. If a student finds that he can avoid having to stay in the isolated area by crying, that is what he will do. If you are going to use this approach, understand ahead of time that you must wait for several minutes of quiet behavior before returning the child to your room. If you will be consistent, the crying in the isolated area will rapidly decrease.

Third, if you have a student who is not particularly fond of math, and he finds out that by misbehaving you will send him from the room, he may well choose the "gloomy" nurse's station over your classroom. At least he doesn't have to do any math. Remember the key factor of location. Before this approach stands a chance of working, the student must want to stay *in* your room. You must try, therefore, to make the classroom as enjoyable as possible for the students.

Fourth, the youngster must remain in the isolated area until you remove him. If you are going to have to continually chase him down the hall, then do not use this approach.

The fifth factor, refers to the behavior pairs, again absolutely critical. If you fail to reinforce an alternatively more appropriate behavior when the youngster is returned to the classroom, you haven't done much for the student. He still may not know how to *avoid* being sent from the room in the future. Therefore, when you do return him to your room, make certain that when you see him behaving appropriately for a few moments or so, you acknowledge the behavior.

Sixth, this approach should work rapidly. If it doesn't, then one of the above factors is either missing or being used incorrectly. If you cannot locate the difficulty (perhaps with the help of a third party), discontinue the approach. Obviously, being out of a classroom for extended periods of time is incompatible with learning the material presented in the classroom.

Charlie

Charlie was quite upset with the fact that his friends had deserted his "cause." He made that perfectly clear by chiding them when they did as the teacher requested. His verbal actions did not move them. His feet, however, did. During the first part of math, he purposely kicked Harry as he placed his feet on the display table. Harry quickly retaliated by pushing Charlie off his chair and onto the floor. Mrs. Tory separated them before a fight started. Harry explained what had happened, and Charlie was once again sent to the vice-principal's office. On the following day, Billy was Charlie's target and, before Mrs. Tory could get to the back of the room, the two boys were punching each other.

"Something is wrong with that boy," Mrs. Tory told the school psychologist. "He doesn't seem to be the least bit affected by my *punishment*. I send him to Mr. Farnum's office and he still comes back doing the same thing."

TWENTY-THIRD YOUDOIT

Question:

1. What would be your reaction to Mrs. Tory's statement that Charlie "doesn't seem to be the least bit affected by my *punishment*?"

a. _____

_____

_____

_____

_____

"Have you talked with Charlie about his behavior?" the psychologist asked.

"I've tried, I've really tried. But he won't say much about it."

"Well, why don't we go see Mr. Farnum. Maybe he can tell us something."

"That's probably not a bad idea," Mrs. Tory replied. "He's seen Charlie more than I have this past month."

TWENTY-FOURTH YOUDOIT

Think about:
1. Charlie's behavior.
2. Mrs. Tory's reaction to his behavior.
3. Possible effects Mr. Farnum is having on Charlie's behavior.

Question:
1. What kind of information would you most likely be looking for regarding what is happening in Mr. Farnum's office?

a. _____

_____

_____

_____

_____

"He's a fine young man," Mr. Farnum said. "Charlie and I have had numerous conversations and I am quite impressed with him. I think he feels the same toward me. Did you know that he has a strong interest in flying? When he found out I have a pilot's license he became very excited."

"Have you been talking with him about flying?" the psychologist asked.

"As a matter of fact, that's all we have been talking about. I even told him I would take him with me the next time I go to the airport to look over a plane I am thinking of renting for a few days."

Dismayed, Mrs. Tory asked, "But you do remember that we talked, and this was supposed to be punishment for Charlie?"

"Oh yes, he and I have talked about his behavior in your class. He assured me that he won't disturb the class anymore. I assumed that he was allowed to come talk with me as soon as he completed his work."

TWENTY-FIFTH YOUDOIT

Recheck your answers to the 23rd and 24th youdoits.

Question:
1. Did your reaction, written in the 23rd youdoit, include the possibility that "punishment" was not being used; that being sent to Mr. Farnum's office was not the same as withholding positive reinforcement?
2. Did Mr. Farnum's explanation provide you with the information you wanted in the 24th youdoit?

TWENTY-SIXTH YOUDOIT

Let's assume that Mrs. Tory needs a new program for Charlie. Your task is to develop one. I will give you some key points that need consideration. I would like you to solve this problem on your own. Afterward, you should take a few moments during class to compare your answers and thoughts. I think I have provided you with enough information enabling you to come up with a plan to reduce the occurrences of foot resting and aggressive behavior Charlie has been manifesting. Before you develop your program, think about the following.
1. Behavior pairs.
2. What will you say to Charlie, if anything, about the new program?
3. How will you influence *both sides* of the behavior pair?

New Program	
Behavior	Environment's Reaction
Desired	Teacher's and/or _____ reaction –
_____	_____
_____	_____
_____	_____
_____	_____

Behavior	Environment's Reaction
Undesired	Teacher's and/or _____ reaction –
(Foot resting; kicking, fighting)	_____
	_____
	_____
	_____

PUNISHMENT IN SCHOOL—ANY JUSTIFICATION?

"I know that we stand a better chance of helping our students if we use a positive approach," Miss Martin reflected. "At the same time, I know that there will be times when our students will do things that will not be good for them in the long run. Whether these things come about as a result of what we or other teachers have done, or what the parents have done, realistically, I am convinced that there are times when punishment will be appropriate, even needed."

"Well, without meaning to hedge," the speaker responded, "before one can agree or disagree with your opinion, you must first carefully define what you mean by the term 'punishment.' Most anything that involves a negative sanction is punishment, at least in the general sense of the word."

"Let's look at a situation when a teacher stops attending to a youngster while he is misbehaving," the speaker continued. "The child is not going to like that very much. For the moment, the situation is unpleasant to him, even punishing. The same holds true for the situation when a teacher prevents one of her students from enjoying an exciting activity because of something he did or didn't do. That's also punishing."

"I see what you are saying," Miss Martin commented. "For me, 'punishment' means corporal punishment; the sort of reaction that Drs. Weingartner and Postman were talking about."

"Well, in all the years that I have been working with schools, teachers, and students," the speaker answered, "I have never found *any* satisfactory justification for the use of physical punishment in our schools. Period! I've seen it used, no question about that. I've heard feeble attempts to justify its use. But the grounds offered for the justification have had little, if any, foundation—at least for me," he quickly added. "I have never met anyone who has been able to convince me that physical punishment belongs in school."

"I must take issue with what you have just said," a man retorted as he abruptly stood up from his seat. "Physical punishment teaches a student respect for his teachers."

"To my knowledge," the speaker stated, looking directly at the man who was standing, "there is no evidence for such an assertion."

"I don't hesitate to use a swift smack to bring some of my kids around," the man answered back. "My kids know this and they respect me."

"Let me answer you this way. There is evidence that suggests that physical punishment does teach students *who* to fear! But I doubt that fear is the same thing as respect."

"They may not be the same," the man responded, "but sometimes you need a little fear before you can learn respect."

"Oh, I didn't know that," the speaker said, with a look on his face that strongly suggested that the man didn't know it, either.

"Yes, and besides, physical punishment helps a child to channel his energies into constructive tasks," the man continued, oblivious to the speaker's facial expression.

"Again, I must say that I know of no evidence for that, either. There is, however, considerable information indicating that it does set up situations where energy is used for destructive purposes."

"But I have seen it work," a young teacher broke in before the man had a chance to say anything further. "I have seen a situation where a firm spanking stopped a third grader's disruptive behavior."

"Did the spanking do anything besides stop the behavior?" someone asked the young teacher. "I mean, how did the punishment effect the child? How did it make him feel toward the teacher who punished him? Did it make him excited about being in school?"

"I don't know about those other things."

"Then I think you must qualify your statement that it worked. All you can say is that it stopped the behavior. And I'm not even certain you can say that. Did it just stop the behavior for that teacher, in that class?"

"I do not know that either," the young teacher answered nervously. "I do recall that the teacher had to punish the child several times for other behaviors in her own classroom. I don't know what happened outside her class."

Sensing that the young lady was in an uncomfortable position, the speaker interjected, "I would like to ask the entire group a question. Assume that the spanking did stop the youngster's disruptive behavior. Would that be sufficient justification for its use?"

"It would be for me," the man who had taken issue with the speaker's earlier statement quickly commented. "If the kid was disrupting the classroom, his antics would have to be stopped. If a spanking would stop him, then fine."

"The issue is not whether the behavior had to be stopped," Anne reacted angrily. "The issue is the approach that was used. Couldn't the teacher have avoided the spanking? Couldn't she have stopped the disruption some other way?" With Anne looking directly at him, the man sat down in his chair.

"You mean by removing a positive reinforcer?" the young teacher said, while turning toward Anne. "In this case, I don't think so. This teacher was so frustrated by this child that I doubt she would have considered anything but the spanking."

"Why was she so frustrated?" Anne asked.

"From what she told me the youngster never did any of his work. He just played around; almost as if he wanted the teacher to get angry at him."

"And did she?"

"Yes. She used to warn him many times that he would be spanked if he didn't behave." (As soon as the teacher finished her statement, quite a few of the teachers in the audience began talking quietly to one another. Some were heard saying that the teacher should never have threatened without carrying through. Others were suggesting that the teacher was attending to the student primarily when he misbehaved.)

"Had he always been that way, I mean at school?" Anne continued. The audience's attention shifted back to the ongoing discussion.

"Apparently not. His previous year's record, although no gem, was satisfactory. But, as I remember, he came into the class pretty far behind the rest of the students."

In the most gentle of voices, Anne said, "It almost sounds as if the child was being punished because he wasn't doing very well in his *schoolwork*."

"No, he was punished because he was being *disruptive*."

"You know, I think we need to answer a very important question," Anne suggested. "Why was he being disruptive in the first place?"

"I'm not following you."

Anne paused for a moment. She looked toward the speaker who, in turn, nodded affirmatively. "Well, you did say that the youngster was pretty far behind in his work. I wonder if that didn't have something to do with his disruptiveness? I mean, if the teacher was frustrated ...dissatisfied, she must have demonstrated her displeasure to the youngster. Unless he was blind, I am certain he picked it up. He knew he was doing poorly, and she may have unintentionally reminded him of that fact several times. He probably received very little positive experience from his work. In fact, he undoubtedly experienced negative things. What was his alternative? One, he could sit for six hours with his hands folded, watching the world go by; two, he could begin to act up a little. He opted for the second behavior. He discovered that he was able to gain some attention from the teacher and probably from his peers as well. Prior to that, he wasn't even noticed."

There were several minutes of silence. The young teacher was holding her head as if in thought. "You are suggesting, I think, that the whole punishment situation could have been avoided had the teacher done something about the youngster's academic difficulties."

"To be honest with you," Anne responded, "I don't know. But I think it is something that needs consideration. I just wonder how the child would have reacted had he experienced some success with his work. Maybe he wouldn't have had to act up to gain attention. Maybe the teacher wouldn't have had to give him any attention for his misbehavior, and it wouldn't have occurred so often."

Again the audience was silent. The speaker walked to the front of the stage and sat down on the floor, looking at the many faces before him. "For the most part," he began, "when we consider physical punishment, we are not talking about stopping behaviors that will result in a student experiencing serious physical harm while at school. Instead, we are talking about chewing gum, talking, running in the halls, throwing paper airplanes, and sassing an authority. These are some of the behaviors that result in physical punishment. I can't help but think that there must be a better way to deal with such actions. A teacher's consistent nonresponse may be enough. Perhaps a brief loss of a privilege would help the student reduce his misbehavior."

"Then you are justifying the use of removal of positive reinforcement to reduce behavior?" a teacher asked.

"Yes, but only with a very important assumption: that you and I are as certain as is humanly possible that *we* are not responsible for the behavior for which the child receives the negative sanction. I'm not only talking about our occasional accidental reinforcement that is given when disruptive behavior occurs. I'm talking about what is actually going on in our classrooms regarding the subjects we are supposed to be teaching. I, like Anne, also wonder what would have happened to the third grader if his teacher had taken the necessary time to guarantee the youngster success with his classwork. If you and I, as teachers, fail to show our students how to achieve success and reinforcement with math, spelling, reading, and other subjects, I do not know why we should expect our students to be anything but 'troublemakers.' Have you ever taken a course at college where the hour spent was wasteful and boring? What did you do during that hour? Write letters? Think about what you were going to do on the weekend? Talk with a neighbor? Draw pictures? Those are examples of 'disruptive' behavior, aren't they? Would you have been as inclined to do those things if the teacher had been stimulating, if the course had been enjoyable, or if you had been experiencing something positive?"

"We are going to have situations that will warrant some negative sanctions," the speaker continued. "To deny that would be too Pollyannaish. But the negative sanctions do not have to be physical. We can accomplish the reduction of misbehaviors through other approaches. But even under the conditions where we do withhold our reinforcement for brief periods of time, we must be willing to look at *our own* behavior. We must be willing to accept the responsibility for what is going on—even if we are not totally responsible for it. If we offer our students little opportunity for success, be it social or academic success, then I strongly believe that we must conclude that something is wrong with us. *We must change* before we can expect our students to change. And punishing our students will not be the answer to bring about that end."

Two Youdoits

I am going to give you a little practice with the various approaches we have discussed up to this point. The cases I will present deal almost exclusively with social behaviors. Think about the ideas we have looked at both for increasing and decreasing behaviors.

TWENTY-SEVENTH YOUDOIT

Harvey's Group

Harvey was the undisputed leader in his eleventh-grade history class. He scored the highest grades on the class tests; he was the tallest member of the class; he was the most vocal member of the class; and he was the most disruptive member of the class. He could elicit more volunteers for mischievous doings than anyone Mrs. Edwards had ever known. He was such an imposing figure that his teacher was reluctant to be assertive in his presence. The situation was complicated by the fact that Harvey's antics were not consistent. On some days, he would be cooperative and pleasant, and so would his group. On other days, he and his cohorts made the Battle of Bunker Hill seem like a picnic.

Mrs. Edwards had tried various ideas to bring order to the classroom when the charge was on. She kept the group and Harvey after school.

She talked with them about how they were disturbing the others in the class. She mentioned that their calling out, their wisecracking, and their "cute" answers to questions only resulted in a lot of wasted time. On other occasions, she would warn the offenders (when they would misbehave during class) that if they continued, they would be sent to the principal's office for discipline, although she never sent them. On still other occasions, she would stop her lecture and require that everyone in the class open their textbooks and read silently. This usually resulted in some open giggling from Harvey's troups which, in turn, resulted in their staying after school.

During the few days that Harvey was absent, the entire class went quite well. Mrs. Edwards would be quick to praise the "leaderless" group under those conditions. As best she could tell, they responded positively to her praise, that is, until Harvey returned to class. Then their behavior would be determined by what Harvey wanted.

Assume you are the teacher. You have a relatively free hand in deciding what you can do; just be realistic. Your goals will be to reduce the amount of influence Harvey has on the group, to increase Harvey's appropriate classroom behavior, to increase his group's appropriate classroom behavior, and to reduce the occurrences of "wisecracking" during class discussion time. Think about behavior pairs for Harvey and the group: which programs you will use to influence both sides of the pairs; how you will implement your programs; and how you will know that your programs have been successful.

_____

_____

_____

_____

_____

_____

_____

_____

TWENTY-EIGHTH YOUDOIT

Beth

Unlike Harvey, Beth was the smallest youngster in her fifth-grade class. If she weighed forty pounds, she did so with bricks in her shoes. She was a wide-eyed, smiling youngster, with an enormous amount of energy. She was also a very good student, academically, that is. Her work was always excellent and, on her "good" days, she would sit for long periods of time solving problems, reading her assignments, and participating in class discussion.

She was, however, not well-liked by her classmates, a situation she brought on herself. She would get into numerous fights (mostly with boys), losing more times than not. In class, she was just as likely to tell someone to shut up when they were answering a question, as to openly compliment them on their answer. When not being attended to by her teacher, she would often groan while holding onto her head or stomach, indicating loudly that if she did not get to the nurse's station immediately, she would probably die. (During one week, she visited the nurse's station nineteen times!) Although requested to do so, she rarely raised her hand if she had something to say. Instead, she would walk up to the teacher's desk and, if she were not attended to at once, she would park herself on top of the desk, and then ask her question. Out of desperation, the teacher would usually respond to her question.

When the class went to the school library, Beth usually created a scene by calling out to another student who was sitting on the opposite side of the library. This resulted in a reprimand from the librarian and a warning that it must not occur again. However, most times, it did.

Whenever possible, her classmates would ignore her antics. They simply were tired of her interruptions and disruptions. Beth would refuse to accept their ignoring her, and a "bothered" student would complain to the teacher eventually.

For the most part, the teacher had tried to help Beth by talking with her when she would be disruptive. The teacher was very concerned that Beth had so few friends, and she felt that she had to be one. Most of the conversations took place immediately after Beth had misbehaved. The teacher would have Beth come to her desk and would ask the youngster to consider the other students and not be so disruptive. This conversation appeared to work for awhile, but soon Beth would start another fracas.

Early in the school year, the teacher had placed Beth in a carrel located in the back of the room when she would start a fight with one of the other students. However, this approach was discontinued because Beth would scream and yell while in the carrel.

No attempt had been made to send Beth to the principal's office. The teacher was very much against this idea because she "knew" that the principal was very punitive.

Beth's parents had been contacted, but they did not wish to be of any assistance. They felt it was the school's problem.

The teacher noticed that Beth really enjoyed being outside. She was an excellent jacks and four-square player. Many of the boys in the class enjoyed playing with her because she was so good. However, "friendships" developed during recess quickly ended when everyone was back in class.

Once again, assume you are the teacher. There are several restrictions under which you will have to work. First, you cannot send Beth to the principal's office. Second, the school Beth attended did not have a specified recess period. The only time the youngsters were allowed outside was during lunch time. They had one hour for lunch and anytime that was not spent for eating could be used for playing outside. There was no way to alter this situation. Third, you will not be able to use the carrel located in the back of the classroom. The teacher said that Beth's protesting made it impossible to teach.

There were thirty-one students in this class. The teacher's approach was reasonably "open." The students were allowed to choose what they wished to work on. There were exceptions to this approach, specifically on the occasion that the teacher had planned a lesson for the students to work on together. Beth was equally disruptive or, at times, equally good, under both conditions.

_____

_____

_____

_____

_____

_____

_____

Consistency

Solving the last two youdoits is much easier here, of course, than in your actual classroom. Writing about what you would do is not quite the same as doing it. Our best laid plans often meet with unexpected situations, and the outcomes of such situations are that our results are not what we intended. Perhaps one of the most difficult, yet important, situations you will have to contend with is your own consistency.

Let me go back to the very beginning of our discussion for just a moment. I think you will see why consistency is so important. One of the basic points we have looked at is the potential amount of influence you will have with your students. Your actions and reactions communicate a good deal of information to your students. They learn what to do and what not to do partly as a result of what *you do*. With this last statement in mind, it should be apparent that the more consistent you are, the more rapidly the appropriate behavior will be learned. Let me offer you a couple of slightly exaggerated examples.

Suppose that we have two teachers, Mary and Jack. They both teach the same children, in the same classroom, at the same time. The lesson for the class this week deals with a simple math problem—how much are two plus two? Mary believes the answer to be *four*, while Jack insists the answer is *five*. (You and I will be watching the behavior of one student, Johnny.)

While Jack is working with other pupils, Mary sits with Johnny and begins to "teach" him to say "four" when asked, "How much are two and two?" The first time the problem is presented, Johnny hesitates briefly. Because he has four brothers and four sisters, he responds, "Four."

"That's right," Mary says, "you are so smart. Two and two are four. I am really pleased. Let's try that once more. How much are two and two?"

Somewhat overwhelmed by Mary's reaction, Johnny repeats his response and is once again showered with praise, affection, and a chocolate chip cookie.

(Somewhat later in the hour, Johnny walks over to Mr. Jack.)

"Hi John," Jack says, "How are you?"

"I'm just great," he answers happily. "You know what?"

"What?"

"I know how much two and two are. They're four!"

"John, I'm sorry, but whoever told you that was wrong. Two and two are not four. Two and two are five. Now go back to your seat and think about that."

"But Ms. Mary taught me the answer. She even hugged me and gave me a chocolate chip cookie."

"Well, I'm sorry," Jack said in a more stern voice. "Your answer is wrong. I am surprised at both you and Mary."

Obviously, the above situation will never take place. But let's look closely at what happened. Johnny has received two distinctly different reactions to his answer. On the one hand, Mary has praised him and confirmed his answer of four. Jack has done the opposite. Mary has "said" to Johnny that in the future, when someone asks you how much two and two are, the answer four is appropriate, and it may be followed by a sign of appreciation. Jack, again, has done the opposite.

If we can define confusion as not knowing quite what to do in situations that appear similar, we would be correct in saying that Johnny is confused. He might ask us, "Which response is right? What do my teachers want me to do?" If he continues to experience these different reactions from his two teachers, the likely outcome will be that he will learn to say "four" when Mary is around and "five" in the presence of Jack. It is difficult to say what he will do if both teachers ask him the *same* question at the *same* time.

Let's change the situation somewhat. Suppose Johnny has as many brothers and sisters as I have suggested. Suppose further that while at home, Johnny has learned that to get something he wants, he has to be a little aggressive. Nothing "serious," just some pushing and grabbing. Since Johnny has learned that these actions usually help him obtain what he wants, he brings the same behaviors into Mary's and Jack's classroom. Mary likes these behaviors. She thinks it is important for young children to be assertive. For her, pushing and grabbing are examples of assertive behavior. On the other hand, Jack sees these same behaviors as potentially dangerous. He believes that they will lead to more aggressive types of actions and, in his view, children are already aggressive enough as it is. Given this information, you and I might observe the following sequence.

Jack has taken some pupils from the room. They are sitting on the grass talking about flowers. Inside the class, Mary is also discussing flowers. The youngsters have been asked to draw their favorite flower. Needing a red crayon, Johnny quickly looks around to find one. He sees one in his friend's hand. With a slight push, shove, and grab, he can now finish coloring his rose. Mary observes this taking place. As Johnny looks in her direction, she smiles and nods her approval. She also reminds Johnny that his friend, if he desires, can take the crayon back, using the same approach. (John whispers to himself, "Fat chance!")

Shortly, the teachers change places. Mary is outside and Jack is now inside. John is a little perturbed. He has just been asked to draw some grass around his rose. Unfortunately, he has no green crayon. He remedies that situation quickly. Jack also observes this taking place. He, too, is perturbed.

"You give that crayon back to Jane this minute," he tells Johnny in a sharp tone. "Because of what you have done, you will not be able to color anymore today. Go take the seat in the far corner. Stay there until I tell you to return. You are never to grab again. Do you understand?"

(Yipe!)

Once again our young friend has received two distinctly different reactions to his behavior. In one instance, Mary has told him it is acceptable to grab, and so forth. She has demonstrated her approval. Johnny now knows what Mary will do.

Jack, on the other hand, has done the opposite. He has shown Johnny that grabbing will result in a loss of privileges and confinement in the back of the classroom. Johnny now knows what Jack will do.

As with the simple math problem, Johnny will have a difficult time knowing what he should do. Again, he will probably choose what to do only after he carefully observes *who* is in the room.

To bring some order out of these two examples, let me combine *Mary* and Ja*ck* and make them one teacher, Mack. Imagine Johnny's situation if Mack responds to the two behaviors as Mary *and* Jack responded. On one day, Mack punishes Johnny for grabbing and, on the following day, he fails to respond in any way to the exact same behavior. Or, Johnny is sent from the room for pushing on Monday, but he is allowed to stay in the room and enjoy the class activity after doing the same thing on Tuesday. Worse still, let's say that Mack "pulls a Mary *and* Jack" on the *same* day, within a fifteen-minute period. Now, either Johnny, or Mack, or perhaps both, are really going to have some problems. "Make up your mind, Mack!" Johnny might say. "Do *me* a favor, would you? Let me know what *you* want me to do!" he might add. Mack, in turn, might respond to Johnny, "Hey, little one, I don't know what I want you to do. I haven't *made up* my mind yet." Or, "Hey, little one, I *feel* differently now than I did fifteen minutes ago. That's why I changed my mind."

Mack's last two statements summarize the two major reasons responsible for our inconsistency: our own indecision and our moods.

DECISIONS

If you don't know what you want your students to do, you can't expect them to know either. And—read this one slowly—if you don't know what you want your students to do, you're not going to know what to do when they do it, because you won't know that they have done it!

Seriously, much of our inconsistency is a result of the mystery and ambiguity often found in our classroom. No one really knows what is expected. You can reduce a good deal of this ambiguity and confusion by getting together with your students and making joint decisions regarding classroom guidelines and potential means for dealing with the guidelines. You will still have plenty of room for spontaneity, creativity, and the spice of the unexpected, but at least everyone will have some idea of their role and responsibility. You should spend several days during the first week of school deciding on these guidelines. Talk about some of the things you believe to be important. Allow your students to do the same. Either incorporate all the suggestions into your classroom approach or compromise. If you desire, make a list of the class' decisions. Talk about these decisions occasionally. Maybe they need to be updated and revised. If you can get your students involved in the decision making, not only will your class run more smoothly, but you will be able to use all of the previously discussed procedures to the greater benefit of yourself and your students. You will be more prepared for things when they happen, both good and not so good. This will help you to be more consistent.

MOODS

From, *Teaching Our Children.*

"A situation pops up which makes us feel on top of the world, or underneath it. Our disposition or mood changes as a result of the situation. Then our students do something and it is only a guess as to how we will react. Whether one has learned to bite his lip, or count to ten, or run outside and kick a weed, the idea is pretty much the same, getting a hold of oneself. Sometimes it works and sometimes it doesn't. . . .

You and I usually know why we are biting our lip, but our students rarely have this information. They just bare the brunt of our reactions. We are the ones who experienced the situation which just set us off, our students may not even know that the situation occurred." (The word students has replaced the word child. Macht, 1975)

I wonder if it would be feasible for teachers to have hurricane flags that could be raised when they felt a storm brewing. We often ask children to sit down, relax, and calm down when they are upset. Why can't teachers be allowed to do the same? (I suspect the working teacher could offer us several very good reasons why it "can't" be done.) If a teacher has a good working relationship with her students, if they are working with her and not against her, then she *can* say to them, "I'm in one of those moods." She *can* ask and receive a brief "break time" before moving ahead. Without it, there is a good chance everyone is going to go down the big hill.

Each time we react to our students' behavior, we are communicating information. To a large degree, our students use our reactions as an indication of what to do in the near future. The more consistent we are, the easier it will be for them to learn what is desired. This rapid learning will be beneficial to everyone. The more often students behave as the teacher desires, the more likely it is that the teacher will be warm, friendly, and understanding. In turn, this means that the teacher will be someone the students will enjoy being with. And you can't beat that!

Cues for
Behavior

"There is a curious thing that often happens in my class. I would like to ask you about it," Miss Martin began. "Why is it that some students do so well one day and so poorly the next? Do you remember, Beth had good days, and Harvey was an 'angel' some of the time, but not others. How is it that a child can be really good in one class, but a real devil in another?"

"What you have described," the speaker answered, "is not uncommon. The same thing can occur at our own home. Some children, for example, are very cooperative and pleasant when Mother is around, but as soon as Grandma enters the picture, boom!"

"Funny that you bring up that example," a second teacher commented. "That's exactly what happens at my house. Have you been over there without my knowing?"

"I don't think so," the speaker answered, smiling.

"You know, now that Kathy has mentioned it," the second teacher continued, "I have, or hopefully had, an unusual situation similar to what she is talking about. There is a little boy in my class who does remarkably well on some days, but on others he is very cranky and sometimes just falls asleep. Recently, I talked with his parents. They are certain that it has something to do with the father's work schedule. Some evenings, Father comes home very late and his entrance often wakes his son. Then the parents have a difficult time getting the child back to sleep."

"Father's entrance, as you have pictured it," the speaker responded, "does appear to be partially responsible, at least, for the youngster's different behaviors in your class. The entrance is often called a setting event. The event literally sets the stage for different types of behaviors to take place. This is very similar to the situation when the two-year old fails to get a good nap in the daytime because someone is mowing the lawn close to his window. The noise and lack of rest are, again, setting events, which as any Mother knows can have quite an influence on the child's behavior for the remainder of the day. Had the setting event not occurred, the youngster probably would have behaved pretty much as usual."

"In my case, at least," the second teacher offered, "I think the problem is solved. Father's work schedule is going to be permanently changed. He won't be working nights any longer."

"You are lucky," the speaker said. "Sometimes there is little we can do about some of these events. I remember a youngster who would come to school and raise the roof on the days his parents argued during breakfast. The parents were urged to avoid such situations, but our urging accomplished little. Fortunately, the youngster's teacher was quite perceptive. He could almost always tell which days the parents argued, and he would arrange to have the youngster do something that would help settle him down. It usually worked."

"Interestingly," the speaker continued, "sometimes these setting events, or cues, as they are also called, that influence behavior do not occur at home or prior to class. They occur right in class. And you and I are the ones who give the cues."

"You mean we set the stage, or cue different types of behaviors?"

"Precisely."

"I'm not certain that I understand," a third teacher said. "Maybe if you could give me an example of what you mean by the word 'cue,' this idea would be more clear."

"I'm sorry, i should have already done that. Let me talk about a traffic light for a moment. That should help. When we drive, a red traffic light acts as a *cue* for us to place our foot on the brake pedal in our car. A green light, on the other hand, suggests that we avoid the brake and use the gas pedal. Neither the green or red light forces us to do what we usually do. Instead, they just set the stage or cue the behavior of using the brake or gas pedal. They actually help us to know when the time is right to do something or not do something. An alarm clock is the same sort of thing. When we look at the time showing on the clock, again, certain behaviors are cued. For example, if we have to be at work by 8:00 a.m. and the clock reads 5:00 a.m., then we can go back to sleep for a couple of hours. However, if the clock says 7:45 a.m., there is a good chance that we will do something other than go back to sleep."

"But we do not have traffic lights and alarm clocks in our rooms, or most of us don't," the third teacher said.

"Probably not. But you do have your facial expressions, your tone of voice, your body positions, and your words. These, and a host of other things, are very powerful cues. They can have a great deal of effect on your students' behavior."

"I see, like a frown or pointing a finger. . . ."

"Or whether you are in or out of the room; or when a substitute takes over the class; or even when a particular student is present or absent. Remember Harvey and his group?"

"In other words," the third teacher said, "when I point my finger at one of my students, that tells him to stop doing whatever he was doing."

"Maybe. You are probably going to need a 'special' look on your face as well. For example, if you smile and point your finger at the same time, perhaps your message will be different than if you frown and point. You see, these cues acquire their information properties as a result of how they have been associated with your reactions in the past. If a youngster has experienced some form of punishment after you have frowned and pointed your finger when he was doing something, then in the future, he may realize that those *same cues* mean that if he doesn't stop, he will be punished again. The cue tells him that now is *not* the time to do whatever he was doing. Let's go back to the traffic light for a moment. Suppose you have never driven before; better yet, you've never even been in a car. The red or green light will be meaningless to you, in the sense of driving, that is. You might think they are left over Christmas decorations. But as soon as you start driving you learn that they serve a purpose. You might learn the hard way; a twenty-five dollar ticket for 'running' a red light can often affect behavior rather quickly. If that happens, there is a good chance that the next time you see an upcoming red light you will stop many feet short of it. Note that the red light cues you as to what to do (and what to avoid doing). You learn to avoid 'running' it, because you have learned that stopping enables you to avoid tickets. The youngster learns that by stopping his misbehavior in the presence of your frown and pointed finger, he, too, can avoid whatever punishing reaction you gave him in the past."

"Let me complicate matters a little," the speaker continued. "Suppose you have a teacher who likes (and *reinforces*) his pupils to raise their hands when they wish to say something. He also fails to attend to or recognize them when they call out without raising their hands. Another teacher, on the other hand, desires, *and reinforces* just the opposite. She prefers her students to call out. She does not respond to them when they raise their hands. With enough experience with these two teachers, a student will know whether or not to raise his hand, if he wishes to be recognized."

"Your term 'experience' means, again, that the student has raised *and*, perhaps, not raised his hand, and has now learned how *each teacher* will respond to his hand raising," the third teacher commented.

"Yes, that is correct. After a few experiences, the student will probably know something about what to do and what not to do in the presence of those two teachers. Remember, however, hand raising is only one, simple behavior."

"I have the feeling that this idea of cues can become very confusing and very complicated for each student," the teacher continued. "After all, he has several teachers and there are many possible behaviors. I can imagine that without some pretty clear cues and some consistent responding on the part of a teacher, a student might really not know what to do."

"I think you also see that with clear cues and consistent responding we can decrease some of the confusion. Imagine what would happen if we let our students know what we expect and then let him know what our probable reactions will be to his behavior in our presence," the speaker asked rhetorically. "The student would know that a specific teacher would be a cue for a specific set of behaviors."

"Let me quickly add that this specificity can accidentally work against a teacher, as well. Let me use Miss Martin as an example of what I mean. Suppose Johnny has learned that in Miss Martin's presence, walking around and disturbing other students will result in Miss Martin *asking* him to stop. On the other hand, Johnny has learned that the same behavior, in Anne's class, results in something different. Anne no longer asks him to stop. Instead, she prevents him from going to the activity center when he walks around and disturbs. Now suppose Johnny likes the attention he receives from Miss Martin; he likes being asked to stop. However, he does not like missing activity period. He, therefore, uses the presence and absence of Miss Martin or Anne to know whether it is 'worth it' to walk around and disturb others. In this example, each teacher cues the youngster that a different reaction will occur for the exact same behavior. The chances are that Johnny will be more likely to walk around and disturb others in the presence of Miss Martin than in the presence of Anne."

"What would happen if I changed the way I reacted to his behavior?" Miss Martin asked.

"Two things would probably change, depending, of course, on what your new reaction would be. First, if your reaction was something Johnny did not like, his disturbing behavior would begin to decrease. Second, your cueing property for that behavior would also change. Johnny would learn that in your presence, walking and disturbing would be reacted to in a less pleasant way. You would now be a cue for something else other than walking and disturbing."

"How about sitting and cooperating?"

"Only if you *reinforce* those behaviors when they occur, *in your presence.*"

"I was afraid you'd say that," Miss Martin said. Then, with only a moment's hesitation, she added, "I think your last statement has just enabled me to answer one of my earlier questions. If a young student is doing something in one class, but not in mine, then maybe it's because the other teacher is reinforcing that behavior in, as you say, his presence, while I am not doing the same thing when the student is with me. If I can find a teacher who is having success with a student I am having difficulty with, I should go watch what he is doing. He must be a cue for that youngster to be doing something, again, while I am not. If I can model myself after him, perhaps, I will be able to help the student behave in about the same way in my class."

"Whether you realize it or not," the speaker began immediately, "you have just hit on one of the more practical and important aspects of this cueing discussion. I think most of us agree that statements such as 'the student *always* does that,' or 'he *never* does that' are usually exaggerations. What the statements more aptly mean is that the student 'never' or 'always' does something in 'my' presence. Usually, if we spend enough time looking, we can find exceptions to the always or never. When we do find the exceptions, it is imperative that we note not only the conditions under which the exceptions take place, but also how the *person,* in the presence of whom the behavior is (or is not) occurring, responds. For example, the child who is extremely hyperactive 'all the time,' can often be found spending many minutes concentrating intensely on something that holds interest for him. Such a youngster might be called 'selectively' hyperactive. Given certain situations he is active; given others, he demonstrates a fairly extended 'attention span.' Another youngster, who 'never' speaks can be found speaking with great frequency given a certain situation, such as being with the teacher instead of in front of a large class. By finding the cueing situation and noting how the environment is influencing the exceptions, we stand an excellent chance of helping the youngster generalize his more appropriate behavior to new cueing situations.

All Children Do That, Except for Those Who Don't

According to Mother, two-year-old Betsy cried all the time. "I guess," she said, "all children her age do the same." Since I knew the parents very well, I said to her, "Yes, all children her age do that, except for those who don't." Her smile indicated that my message was clear.

I met with Betsy's parents and asked them to spend five days counting the number of times Betsy cried; the length of time she cried; the conditions under which she cried (cues); and, how each parent reacted to the crying when it occurred. After the five days of observation and recording, we met again and talked.

The first apparent observation was that Betsy did *not* cry all the time. In fact, she rarely cried *in the presence* of her father. When she did cry when alone with Father, the crying lasted only a few moments. The second thing that we noticed was that Betsy did cry a good deal whether alone with Mother or when both Mother and Father were present. "Why does she cry so often for me and so little for him?" Mother asked, as she pointed a finger toward her smiling husband. "And don't say I told you so, either," she warned him, while returning his smile.

"Based on the information you have given me, it appears that you and Dad do not respond to Betsy's crying in the same way," I began. "Your diary speaks for itself. Notice that for the most part, you respond favorably to Betsy when she is crying. You comfort her; pick her up, and usually give her what she wants while she is crying. Father, however, does not appear to respond to the crying at all, again based on this diary."

"At least, when I know that she isn't hurt or upset," Father added. Then he took the diary, looked it over quickly, and gave it back to me. "Look at the third page. My Betsy is a smart little one. That was the day that she fell off her rocking horse. There was no way she could have hurt herself. We spent a fortune making that carpet soft. Do you know what she did when she fell? *Before* she started to cry, she looked to see *who* was in the room. Who did she see? Momma! Then she started to cry. Not right away, mind you, but only after she saw that her mother was close by. Now, that's smart! She knows what I do most of the time when she cries; she also knows what Mom does 'all' the time when she cries. So, before she decides to spend the effort, she looks to see if her effort will be worthwhile. That day, the answer was yes, because her mother was there."

"So, Mother was a cue for crying, while Father was a cue for not crying?" the teacher asked.

"In this case, yes. Betsy had learned how her environment would respond to her crying, most of the time, anyway. She had also learned how to predict what response she would get when crying."

"By seeing which cue was present?"

"Right. Since Mother wished to reduce the frequency of this attention-getting crying, she was told to avoid attending to that type of crying and asked to attend to Betsy's noncrying as much as possible."

"Then the cueing situation changed automatically, didn't it?" the teacher asked.

"Yes. As soon as Mother changed the way she responded to the behavior, her presence became a cue for the more preferred noncrying."

"Because she now reinforced the noncrying?" Miss Martin asked.

"Right."

"What you are saying," Miss Martin continued, "is that we can help ourselves and our students by making our cues clear, our reactions consistent, and our desires known. We can make our classroom less mysterious that way."

"Yes, that's pretty much what I am saying. We ask our students to make some difficult discriminations, to know when the time is right to do certain things. I think we can help them a great deal by making our cues meaningful, by talking about some of the things we expect, by reminding our students of the probable consequences to their actions, and by being as consistent as we can in regard to the cues and our reactions."

"Let me ask you this," he continued. "Have you ever driven in an unfamiliar city where the street signs were new and meant nothing to you? You didn't know whether to turn right or left. There were no clear cues. Making the wrong turn could be fairly punishing. You could have literally gone around in circles for hours. You probably. . .eventually, found your way around, although you might have had to ask someone what was the right thing to do. Well, the same thing can happen to our students, and right in our own classrooms."

Skill Learning and the Classroom Teacher

Stereotaxic Implantation — What Did You Say?

For the next fifteen minutes, I would like you to write on a piece of paper a 500-word description of a stereotaxic implantation. I want you to be very specific and complete. (By the way, your grade in the course you are now taking is solely dependent on your answer. If you fail to give an adequate answer, by my standards, you will have to stay after school until the assignment is completed. Lots of luck!)

"I have never heard of that thing," a teacher volunteered. "I'm not even certain that I can spell it."

"Well," the speaker said as he paused to close his notes, "if you've never heard of the term, and you can't spell it, then I guess it is not fair of me to ask you to write about it, is it?"

"Does it have something to do with listening to records?"

"Nope, that's wrong."

"At least I know that it has nothing to do with records. Are you going to tell us?" the same teacher asked.

"If I don't forget, I will. But first, let's look at what I have just done. I have asked you a question that *I* believe you should know. I have also told you that your final grade (earlier your money) depends on your answer. By my actions, I may have unintentionally guaranteed you a taste of failure. At the very least, I have made things uncomfortable for you. Perhaps, I have done a lot worse. I may have turned you off to me, my 'subject matter,' and ultimately, yourself. Hopefully, you are saying that what I have done is unfair, unreasonable, and a few other more choice words. If so, you would be right. Well, without meaning to be too obtrusive, there is a chance that you are unknowingly doing the *same thing* in your own classroom."

"I just don't see how," the teacher responded.

"Let me try to show you," the speaker answered. "Suppose I give you a book to read. Unfortunately, instead of being written in English, the book is written in Greek. Not too many of you will get by the first sentence, much less the first page. Now suppose that you and I give one of our fourth graders a book to read. The book is written in English. The problem is that the youngster's reading level is just barely at the first grade. For him, the fourth-grade book *will* appear as if it is written in Greek. If we ask him to read the following, 'The weather struck with such a force that it made his lips and fingers lame,' his chances for success are about as slim as yours, if you were required to read and *understand,* 'A yogh is a letter used in the writing of Middle English to represent a palatal fricative or a velar fricative.' "

"If that was asked on a true-false test, at least I would have a fifty-fifty chance of getting it right," the teacher reacted. "Seriously, I think I have your point. If we ask one of our students to do something, something that he has never experienced, never heard about, or never read about, it is not likely that he would be able to do what we ask of him."

"Which, in essence, is the same as saying that it is unlikely that he will gain much reinforcement from either us or the subject matter, right?" Miss Martin asked.

"Thank you Miss Martin, that is exactly right," the speaker responded.

"Then I guess that if the student is placed in that kind of a nonsuccess situation for any length of time, we're going to have a troublemaker on our hands," the first teacher said.

"Not only is there a good chance of that happening, but there is a better chance that you are going to have an unhappy student on your hands," the speaker answered.

"It's kind of funny, but I have thought about this before," another teacher offered. "I can remember a few of my college classes. In some cases, I was lost before the professor had talked more than five minutes.

He was so far over my head that I had no idea what he was saying. That happened even when I *had taken* the 'necessary' prerequisite course. When it happened, I can remember being very upset. I think a couple of times I just dropped the class."

"What you have just said brings up a very important point," the speaker commented. "You said it happened 'even when you had taken the necessary prerequisite course.' I believe it might be more accurate to say that it happened even though you *had enrolled* and *sat* in on the prerequisite course."

"I don't think I'm following you," the teacher indicated.

"Let me try to explain. This is very critical. The fact that you sat in on the course does not tell us how much you learned from that course, agreed?"

"Agreed."

"It is possible, therefore, that two or twenty-two students could have taken the same course, sat in the class for the same amount of time, and each could have come out of the experience with varying degrees of information. Some, then, would be more prepared for a following, sequential course, than others."

"Also agreed."

"So, saying that you had the necessary prerequisite course is not the same as saying that you *learned* the necessary prerequisite *information.*"

"I understand now," the teacher remarked. "Occupying a chair and learning are not the same. I know exactly what you are going to say next. The fact that a pupil has been promoted from first, to second, to third grade, which are, so to speak, prerequisites for fourth grade, does not mean that he has learned the material presented in those first three grades. He sat in his chair, but his records or grades will not always show how much he learned. . . ."

"Or how much new material he is prepared to handle."

"So, if we ask the fourth grader to read a fourth-grade book, *because* he is enrolled in fourth grade, and he has not learned the necessary prerequisite skills in the earlier grades, that fourth grade book may look like Greek," the teacher thought out loud.

"Absolutely correct. And the very thing you have described happens more times than not. Think about this next idea. I am sure you will agree with me. For the most part, we promote our young students on the basis of *time, not* on the basis of *performance.* If a first grader has sat in his seat for approximately 183 days, if he has learned, perhaps, no more than 50 percent of our material, and if he is a pretty good kid, whatever that means, we promote him to second grade. In second grade, if the youngster has sat in his seat for approximately 183 days, if he has learned, perhaps, 50 percent of the material presented to him and, if he again is a good kid, we promote him to third grade. In third grade, if the sequence is repeated, we send him to fourth grade. Now, if not before, we have a potentially serious problem. What will happen if the fourth-grade teacher makes the assumption that the younster has *successfully* completed the first three grades; if she assumes that he has acquired close to 100 percent of the information presented in those grades? What will happen if she operates on that assumption without checking it out? What are the youngster's chances for success? What will happen if she gives the pupil a 'Greek' reading book, a 'Greek' math book, and a 'Greek' science book? Well, what will happen is what happened when I asked you to explain a stereotaxic implantation— nothing. And, in this case, nothing is bad! Our student is going to learn 'nothing,' he is going to read 'nothing.' and he is going to do 'nothing,' except maybe get himself in a little bit of trouble. The more trouble he gets into, the less interested he becomes in school. The less interested, the less work. The less work, the further behind. The further behind, the more trouble he gets into."

"Not a very pleasant or optimistic cycle," the speaker continued as he once again sat down at the front of the stage. "It takes its toll," he said quietly as he looked at Miss Martin, Anne, and the rest of the now familiar faces. "And sadly, you and I perpetuate that cycle year after year."

PRESENT PERFORMANCE LEVEL

The speaker's staring eyes and somber, trailing voice, did nothing to ease the silence that hung heavy over the group. Most everyone in the audience either stared back at him or looked down at their laps. After many minutes, Anne stood up. "That present performance level thing is the key, isn't it? If it is exactly what it sounds like, it will help us to know where our fourth grader *really is* in regard to his work. It will tell us where we must begin our teaching program if we are to offer him an opportunity to experience success. It will help us break that cycle," she said, as she sat down. Then, as if on a spring, she stood back up. "This means that we may have to individualize a program for each student, otherwise we may begin or proceed at a level well above or below his present skills."

As soon as Anne sat down, the speaker got up and walked to the side of the stage where he picked up a piece of chalk and began writing on the portable blackboard. The shuffling of papers could be heard throughout the auditorium as the teachers began writing down what was being presented.

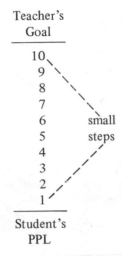

"Anne's analysis of the present performance level," the speaker began, as he pointed to the PPL on the chalkboard, "was perfect. It tells us where our students are in reference to our general or specific classroom goal," he continued, this time pointing to the word "goal." "When we know these two points, the PPL and the goal, what we need to do is to figure a means of helping the students move from their present performance level to our goal. These numbers," he said as he ran the chalk from the numbers one to ten, "represent the small steps or gradual increments of difficulty that actually bridge the gap between the PPL and the goal. These numbers are the real heart of the matter. They are your teaching methods. We will come back to the goal and the small steps in a few minutes. For now, let's concentrate on the present performance level."

"Suppose," he continued, "that thirty students come into a classroom. Let's assume that it is a fourth-grade math class. I assure you the grade could be kindergarten or twelfth, just as well. Of the thirty students, we will say that twenty of them come into the class with about the same amount of information regarding the subject matter that is to be presented in this fourth-grade class. These twenty, as a result of their previous experiences, have the necessary skills to succeed at the beginning fourth-grade level. However, of the remaining ten, five, again because of the experiences they have had, are much more advanced in this subject area than their twenty-five classmates, and five are considerably deficient in their prerequisite knowledge and thus are well below their fellow classmates." The speaker returned to the blackboard as he described his example. He erased the PPL and exchanged the words "difficulty level" for the "small steps."

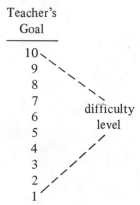

"For clarity," the speaker began, "we will let the number four represent the difficulty level the teacher believes all the students should be ready for. In other words, since *all* the youngsters are about ten years old and have completed first, second, and third-grade math, they *should* be, according to the teacher, prepared to handle the work at the fourth level of difficulty. Unknown to the teacher, however, all the youngsters do not come into her class with the same amount of prerequisite knowledge. Five are closer to level one, and five are ready to handle math work at the seventh or eighth level of difficulty."

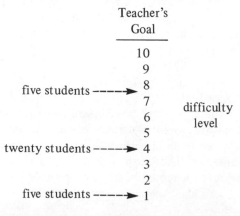

"To make my point, I will say that prior to the introduction of her new work, which will eventually lead to her goal, our teacher does *not* determine the present performance level of her thirty students. Instead, she assumes that they are all ready for the fourth level of difficulty. Any guesses as to what will happen?"

"The five students at level one aren't going to know what she is talking about," one teacher offered.

"And the other five, the ones at the seventh level, are going to be bored," another answered.

"What are the chances of those two groups gaining much reinforcement from their work?" the speaker asked.

"Well," the first teacher began, "I would say that the lower group stands much less of a chance than the upper group. Although, if the upper group is, in fact, bored with what is going on, they won't get much enjoyment from their work, either."

"Okay, fine. Would you suggest to our teacher that she begin her presentation at the same level for all her students, such as saying, 'Everybody turn to page 37, and we will begin?' "

"She could, of course," the first teacher continued, "but, by doing so, she is probably going to lose several of her students right from the start."

"What, then, is her alternative?" the speaker asked the first teacher.

"Obviously to start her program at the point at which each of her students have demonstrated competency; at each student's present performance level. I hear myself saying that," the teacher continued, "but do you know what that means? That means we may have thirty individual programs going on at the same time in our class."

"That's what it means," the speaker responded. "But what is the alternative?"

"I don't know," the teacher answered.

"I don't think it is as bad as it sounds," Anne quickly interjected. "Given the example, that teacher may only have to contend with three, perhaps, four different programs. And they aren't really different. One will have to be less complicated than the others. One will be more complex and challenging. They will be dealing with similar subject matter, just at different levels of difficulty."

"But then you have the situation of 'dummy groups.' You know what some students will do with that label," the first teacher said.

"That shouldn't be much of a problem," a new teacher spoke out. "I have my class divided into sections, depending on how much knowledge they demonstrate in math. During the first few days, when the groups were being set up, I heard some comments from the better prepared students about the 'dummies' sitting at the 'dumb' table. I quickly let them know that that type of conversation would not be tolerated. I explained that some people have had more experience with certain things than others and, as a result, know a little bit more about those things. I further said that that fact does not mean that someone is necessarily more intelligent, but again, more experienced. Then I took the two students who had made the comments and brought them to the front of the class. They were asked to sit down at my desk in full view of their classmates. I told them that the three of us were going to take a test to 'see who knew more.' 'That's not fair,' they said, pointing out that I was the teacher and that, of course, I knew more. I agreed with them but, at the same time, I told them that the main reason why I knew more was because I had much more experience then they did. I never had much of a problem after that," the teacher said.

"That approach is certainly worth a try," the first teacher said. Then, pointing toward the blackboard, she continued, "If I understand you correctly, the ten numbers represent sequential levels of difficulty. Level one is the easiest, level ten, or whatever the highest number, is the most difficult. The teacher determines the present performance level of each student and assigns them to a level at which they are most likely to experience success and demonstrate proficiency."

"That is right," the speaker answered. "Here, I'll show you. Twenty students come in at level four, which is their measured present performance level."

Teacher's
Goal
___

10

9

8

7

6

5

PPL------►4

Twenty
students

"Five come in at level one."

Teacher's Goal	Teacher's Goal
10	10
9	9
8	8
7	7
6	6
5	5
PPL ----►4	4
	3
Twenty	2
students	PPL ----►1
	Five
	students

"Five come in at level seven."

Teacher's Goal	Teacher's Goal	Teacher's Goal
10	10	10
9	9	9
8	8	8
7	7	PPL ---►7
6	6	
5	5	Five
PPL ---►4	4	students
	3	
Twenty	2	
students	PPL ----►1	
	Five	
	students	

"For most subjects," the speaker began, "the present performance level is relatively easy to determine. To show you how to do this, I need to mention something about the teacher's goal. Keep in mind that the PPL is a measure of how much of the teacher's goal the students have attained as a result of their past schooling. In order for a teacher to obtain this measure she is first going to have to make some decision about what she intends to do in class."

"You mean, whether she will teach math or reading," the first teacher commented.

"Yes, but a little bit more than just math or reading, in general. If it is a math class, she may think in terms of subtraction, but she will have to consider subtraction with or without regrouping and how many digits will be involved. If it is reading, she will consider reading level, word recognition, word family rules, pronunciation, comprehension, and the like. In other words, her goal will have to be specific. Her goal should be stated in observable terms, preferably with some numerical value attached (i.e., number of words read, number of problems to be correctly completed). The main purpose for an observable goal is that both she and her students will know when the goal has been reached."

"I'm a little confused about this," the teacher said. "This goal, is it a long- or short-range goal?"

"Probably a combination of both," the speaker responded. "Ideally, she should operate on daily or weekly goals, minigoals if you wish. She could have a long-range goal, for example, to improve reading to the fourth-grade level, but she will need minigoals within that long-range goal; increased vocabulary from 100 to 200 words and more accurate skills in pronunciation (decreasing errors), which can be accomplished or worked on daily."

"Could the minigoals actually be those small steps of increasing difficulty?" the teacher asked.

"Absolutely. In fact, you are several jumps ahead of me. For the most part, the small steps are minigoals. They are parts of the bridge that take the student from his PPL to your determined major goal. Again, I'll come back to this in just a moment. Let's assume that you have a good idea of what you would like to cover during the following week or weeks. Now, you will determine how much of this information the students have prior to your teaching. This will give you an estimation of the students' PPL regarding your goal. You develop a test, written or oral, that will present questions to your students covering an adequate sample of the material you intend to cover. Again, if you are working on subtraction, you might give them fifty problems that range from very simple to those even more complex than you intend to present. The 'test' is *not* graded and the students should know this. They should be told that this test will help you know how much they know so that you will be better prepared to help them. If it is a reading class, the students should be given samples of reading material well *below* their present grade level (or predicted grade level), *at* their present level, and *above* their present level. More than likely, this will be done on an individual basis, whereas math, translation of foreign language, composition, and so forth can be tested on a group basis. I know that you are saying that this will take time. It will, but it is time extremely well spent. You might find that several of your students know as much as you do about the upcoming subject matter. There is no sense in asking them to do something that will put them to sleep. Instead, you will have to challenge them with something more complex and interesting. On the other hand, of course, you may find that several of your students are in no way prepared to deal with what you intend to talk about. You need to find this out ahead of time, otherwise the long-range effects could be catastrophic."

"The measured present performance level will not be perfect. But it will help you discern where your students *are*. By knowing this, you might be able to help a student experience something novel, success."

SMALL STEPS

"Now we come to the most exciting and challenging part of teaching. If we have done our job so far, we have a clear and objective statement of what we would like our students to do—our goal. We also have an estimate of how close each student is to our goal—their present performance levels. Our next task: to bridge the gap from where a student *is* to where we want him *to be*—our small steps."

THIRTIETH YOUDOIT (optional)

If you want to get the feel of what I mean by small steps, and their importance in successfully teaching complex tasks, try to find a willing three-year old and "teach" him to tie his shows. If you can't find a three-year old, take a pair of shoes (with laces, of course!) and put them in front of you. Untie the shoes, and begin to write down each component of shoe tying. For example, "I take the right lace with my right thumb and middle finger and I move the lace to the left, etc." How far left? What is left? It is an unbelievable task. Try it, Don't be surprised if you end up with 150 small steps.

"Each step represents a skill that is needed before a student can accomplish a complex goal. Think of these small steps as rungs on a ladder. To move from the bottom to the top of the ladder, a student must learn each rung. The rung from which the student starts is his present performance level. Again, we will assume that he enters the math class at rung (or level of difficulty) number four."

Teacher's
Goal
_____

10
9
8   difficulty
7   level
6
5
PPL –––––––► 4

"Since the student has demonstrated competency at level four, his next task is to successfully complete step five. Ask yourself, 'What does the student need to know in order for him to move from step four to step five?' What skills will he need? When he accomplishes the necessary skills at level five, he is ready to move to step six. Again the question is asked, 'What does he need to know in order for him to move from step five to step six?' This type of approach continues until he reaches the major goal. Let me give you an example of this entire operation."

"Suppose that successfully solving twenty-five three-digit subtraction problems that include some regrouping (or 'taking away') is a teacher's major goal for her students. Since she is not familiar with her students' present skills regarding this goal, she gives them a present performance level test. A sample of her problems would look like this."

6	9	7	4	12	15	13	27	24	52	86	65	65	75
-4	-2	-6	-0	-1	-3	-5	-4	-7	-6	-5	-8	-18	-43

67	127	134	258	472	853	782
-28	-6	-21	-49	-281	-564	-304

"For the sake of brevity, we will only look at three students. The first student gives the following answers to the above problems."

6	9	7	4	12	15	13	27	24	52	86	65	65	75
-4	-2	-6	-0	-1	-3	-5	-4	-7	-6	-5	-8	-18	-43
10	11	12	4,	3	18	18	11	14	56	81	63	63	48

```
  67    127    134    258     472     853     782
 -28     -6    -21    -49    -281    -564    -304
 ----   ----   ----   ----   ----    ----    ----
  88    123    155    299     683     567     306
```

"The second student answers this way."

```
  6     9     7     4    12    15    13    27    24    52    86    65    65    75
 -4    -2    -6    -0    -1    -3    -5    -4    -7    -6    -5    -8   -18   -43
 --    --    --    --    --    --    --    --    --    --    --    --    --    --
  2     7     1     4    11    11     8    23    17    46    81    57    47    32
```

```
  67    127    134    258     472     853     782
 -28     -6    -21    -49    -281    -564    -304
 ----   ----   ----   ----   ----    ----    ----
  39    121    113    209     191     289     478
```

"Finally, the third student answers this way."

```
  6     9     7     4    12    15    13    27    24    52    86    65    65    75
 -4    -2    -6    -0    -1    -3    -5    -4    -7    -6    -5    -8   -18   -43
 --    --    --    --    --    --    --    --    --    --    --    --    --    --
  2     7     1     4    11    12    12    23    23    54    81    63    53    32
```

```
  67    127    134    258     472     853     782
 -28     -6    -21    -49    -281    -564    -304
 ----   ----   ----   ----   ----    ----    ----
  41    121    113    211     211     311     482
```

"During her years of teaching, the teacher has developed what she considers to be reasonably accurate sequential steps that represent the ladder of basic skills needed to accomplish the goal of twenty-five three-digit subtraction problems, with and without regrouping. These are her steps or difficulty levels."

Step one: identification of number symbols (3, 9, 2, etc.).
Step two: demonstrating knowledge of the concept of place value (47—is this four tens and seven ones?).
Step three: recognition of addition sign (+).
Step four: operation of addition (2 + 2 = 4).
Step five: addition with one digit plus one digit (2 + 2 = 4).
Step six: addition with one digit plus two digits (2 + 35 = 37).
Step seven: addition with two digits plus two digits (34 + 10 =44).

Step eight:	addition with two digits plus three digits (35 + 234 = 269).
Step nine:	addition with three digits plus three digits (457 + 231 = 688).
Step ten:	addition with "carrying" (repeat steps six, seven, eight, and nine).
Step eleven:	recognition of subtraction sign (-).
Step twelve:	operation of subtraction without regrouping, one digit minus one digit (6 - 3 = 3).
Step thirteen:	operation of subtraction without regrouping, two digit minus one digit (27 - 4 = 23).
Step fourteen:	operation of subtraction without regrouping, two digits minus two digits (34 - 11 = 23).
Step fifteen:	operation of subtraction without regrouping, three digits minus two digits (653 - 31 = 622).
Step sixteen:	operation of subtraction without regrouping, three digits minus three digits (743 - 620 = 123).
Step seventeen:	operation of subtraction with regrouping (repeat steps thirteen, 36 - 8 = 28; fourteen, 45 - 28 = 17; fifteen, 621 - 42 = 579; sixteen 852 - 661 = 191).
Step eighteen:	proof (27 - 11 = 16; 16 + 11 = 27).

"The teacher may have to add or delete several steps, depending upon what she observes when working with her students. But notice that as the step numbers increase, the difficulty and complexity increase. Notice, also, that the increase is very gradual. The student should experience little difficulty moving from one step to the next."

THIRTY-FIRST YOUDOIT

Look carefully at the present performance level results from our three students. Given the fact that there are seventeen steps of increasing difficulty (we won't worry about the eighteenth step), see if you can determine at what level our three students should be placed.

Student one   Level number _____

Student two   Level number _____

Student three   Level number _____

"Hopefully, having looked at the three students' answers, you discovered that our teacher will not be able to start her presentation of subtraction at the same level for each of them. If she does, what do you think will happen?" the speaker asked his audience.

"As I said earlier," the first teacher volunteered, "she is going to lose at least one right from the start."

Getting Behavior Started

"And as I said earlier," Miss Martin added, "it is unlikely that at least one of the students is going to gain much reinforcement from the subject matter."

"Again you both are correct. Please understand that the purpose of the approach I am presenting is to offer you an idea that I believe will maximize the chances that each and every student will gain some reinforcement from his work *and* from his teacher. I know that what I am asking you to consider will be time consuming. I know that you have many students to work with, not just one or two, and that you may have several programs operating at the same time. But, in the same breath, as I said earlier, you have the responsibility to guarantee each and every student an opportunity for success. I feel strongly that these ideas of present performance level, of small steps, and clearly stated goals, will increase your chances for fulfilling that guarantee."

"Sometimes," the speaker continued, "you and I expect too much from our students. Sometimes, we fail to offer them encouragement along the way. Instead, we withhold our recognition and positive attention until they reach our desired goal. Some of them never reach it and thus some of them never gain much recognition, even though they have put out considerable effort. To expect our students to continue to persist in the face of no reinforcement is foolhardy. You and I wouldn't do it. Why then, should they? Yet this is the position we often put our students in when we fail to reinforce them for gradual improvement, for gradual progress. This is what we do when we withhold our reinforcement until they attain 'perfection.' Do you know what often happens when we continue to withhold our reinforcement? Our students stop working. And, as cycles often go, another thing happens. You and I assume, after our students *stop* working, that the *absence* of behavior is the same as the *inability* to behave. That assumption is so wrong, it hurts! Simply because a youngster is not doing something does not mean that he *can't* do it. It may be that he sees no reason for doing! I assure you that if that student has experienced failure time in and time out; if he has received little or no recognition despite his efforts; if there is nothing intrinsically enjoyable about his work; and if there is no extrinsic reinforcement offered, then he is *right* when he sees little reason for doing. I will ask you again, what will happen to a student if we start him at level four, if we withhold our reinforcement until he reaches level ten, and if he comes into our classroom at level one?"

"Used correctly, the approach I have offered will prevent such a thing from happening. We do not start a student at a point that he is not ready to handle. We do not withhold our reinforcement until he reaches our goal. Instead, we start him at *his* present performance level, no matter where it may be. We make every effort within our ability to reinforce him as he gradually moves from step to step. Time becomes much less a factor. Performance becomes the major issue. When he succeeds, no matter how long it takes, he will experience something that he might not otherwise experience, regardless of time."

> **KEY:** If there is ever a question of "inability," it is critical that the teacher determine whether a student's absence of behavior is "caused" by the absence of prerequisite skills or the absence of a reason for him to put out effort—positive reinforcement.

"But aren't there times when it is appropriate and correct to conclude that a student simply is not capable of performing some task, that even with all our effort, a student will not be capable of reaching some goal?" Miss Martin asked.

"That is a question that must be answered with the greatest of care. I would like to quickly answer, 'No.' Perhaps, from the purist's viewpoint, 'No' would be the only answer. But the pragmatist would probably concede the answer to be 'Yes.' We do not have unlimited time, unlimited resources, and unlimited personnel, given today's approach to schooling. If we did, we might be able to do most anything. As I see it, a student will be able to succeed only at what he is capable of. The problem is that today, right now, we do not know too much about capacity. Therefore, we do *not* know how much a child is capable of. Any goal, for example, is a reasonable goal, as long as it is appropriate within a student's limitations. Again, however, we just do *not* know too much about limitations."

"The truth is, we are ignorant. But there is nothing wrong with admitting ignorance," the speaker continued. "At times, it is the most intelligent thing we can do. But such an admittance is often very difficult. Man, in general, seems to be reluctant to say, 'I don't know.' He seems compelled to offer some kind of an answer, regardless of whether he has a basis for his answer, and regardless of the long-range effect of his answer. In the field of education, this compulsion can have a most detrimental effect on students. It not only closes doors, it locks them shut. Saying that a youngster is incapable of performing a task, that he is unable to do what is requested, is an example of such an answer. To be true, it must be supported with unquestioning evidence. Yet, because of our ignorance, we rarely have that type of evidence. Despite that we still offer that statement. When the statement goes unchallenged, when it is accepted as truth, in the face of no support, we not only lock out an educational future, we conveniently avoid facing our ignorance. We say, 'something is wrong with the *student,*' and we somehow think that the shifting of responsibility washes our hands clean. Well, it doesn't."

"Our ignorance could be our most powerful impetus, and the elimination of ignorance, our most powerful reward. Have you ever taken a youngster beyond the point at which you were told he was incapable of going? Pretty hard to match the resulting feeling. By doing so, you found a way that had not been found before and you chipped away a small piece of ignorance. You also kept an educational future ajar."

"A few moments ago, I suggested that the small steps are the most exciting and challenging part of teaching. They are the means by which we can bring the 'unattainable' a drop closer. They are our chisels and our doorstops. They can turn failure into success."

THE FIRST SMALL STEP

"Suppose your goal for a particular youngster was to guarantee him some form of reinforcement for a correct answer. How would you be almost 100 percent sure of reaching that goal?"

"Find out something he knows. Then ask him a question about it," Anne suggested. "When he answers the question, praise him or give him some positive attention."

"Simple as that," the speaker responded. "Now suppose that you wish to guarantee the same student a successful experience in a particular subject matter area. How would you do it?"

"The same way," Anne answered once again. "Find out his present performance level. Then have him do something that he has already successfully demonstrated."

"Beautiful. Let me quickly ask you this. Who is going to feel better, the student who succeeds right from the start, or the student who tastes failure before he reaches first base? Who is going to be more likely to come back for seconds? Who, perhaps, will feel more confident and self-assured?" Without waiting for answers, the speaker continued. "The first step serves three basic functions: first, to move the youngster a little closer to the teacher's desired goal; second, to clearly demonstrate to the student that the teacher will react in a positive way to his correct responses; third, to guarantee the student a taste of success. Once again," looking in the direction of Anne, the speaker asked, "how do we guarantee the student a taste of success?"

"We begin working with him at, or ever so slightly above, his present performance level," she answered.

"And we reinforce him immediately after his correct answers," the speaker quickly added. "By doing so we get him started on a positive note. All initial responses, no matter how small and no matter how far away they might be from the ultimate goal, should be followed immediately by some warm, animated, positive reaction from the teacher. Okay, how about the second small step?"

"My guess is," Miss Martin began, "that it should be a little bit more complex than the first, that it should be somewhat closer to the goal."

"That's right, and it, too, should be accompanied by the teacher's praise," the speaker said. "The third step, fourth step, and so on, will again move in the direction of the goal, although the moving will be gradual and based exclusively on the student's performance. We adjust our steps to fit the student."

"Sometimes, however," continued the speaker, "what appears to be a good 'fit' from our viewpoint turns out to be inadequate. Assume that you have a good estimate of each of your students' present performance levels. As a result, you have either divided them into groups, you have assigned individual material from a work book, or you are working with certain students on a more or less one-to-one basis. You are well-liked by your students, and they respond favorably to your demonstrated affection and praise. Everything is going fine. All of a sudden, one of your students begins to falter. His gradual improvement has ceased. He seems to be stuck at a particular level of difficulty and, despite your encouragement, he no longer is progressing. How might you account for such a situation?"

"He could be tired," one teacher offered. "He might not have slept well the night before, or he could have played really hard during recess. It does happen," she added.

"Okay, there is one possibility," the speaker answered. "How about another."

"In your example, it appears that the teacher is relying on social reinforcement. It might be that it has lost some of its effectiveness. She might need to use something else, like a few minutes of extra free time," a second teacher suggested.

"That could be checked out," Anne said. "The teacher could have the student do something else, something that he had done previously. When it was successfully completed, she could praise him and see how he responds to it. That might not always work, but she might get some idea from it."

"There is something else I would certainly wish to check out," Anne continued. "I doubt that any two students are exactly alike. So I doubt that any singular program will be sufficient for all students. It could be that this student, the one who has stopped progressing, needs some more help. For example, if he successfully accomplished step five, but he continually failed to achieve the sixth one, perhaps you need an in-between step. A step "five a" might be just enough to help him learn number six."

"I know you are not going to like this," another teacher said as she stood up," but it may be that this student simply cannot go any further. You could have steps "five a" and "five b" and "five c" and it still might not help. For some unknown reasons, he just can't make it. Realistically, I believe that is a possibility. As his teacher, I would hate to put him in a situation that would frustrate him. That might wipe out all the positive things I had done before."

"I can't deny that the possibility exists," the speaker answered. "At the same time, I would like to ask you what you would do if you were faced with the situation?"

"If I had done everything I could, given my experience and training," the teacher answered, "I would try to find someone who was a little more trained and experienced. I would ask him for help."

"And I would do the same," the speaker responded. "I think that is what we should all do. We have limitations. Recognizing and operating within these limitations is, perhaps, the most favorable thing we can do for our students. Remember, by asking others for help, we keep the door open. That is a far cry from saying that a student can't do it and dropping the matter there. Interestingly, if another person does help the student, it is probably because he or she was able to develop a step "five a" that you and I would never have considered."

"Again, we are talking about individualization, aren't we?" Anne asked.

"That's right," the speaker responded. "Therein lies the challenge. The development of additional steps that help the student acquire something with which he is having trouble is an exciting undertaking. You will find yourself taxing your experience and training. How do I present the material so he can grasp it, you may ask? What does he need to know to understand the concept? What part of the puzzle is missing? How do I help him discover it? When you find the answers to these and other questions and the youngster, in fact, begins to move again, his excitement and enthusiasm will sustain *your* efforts for many moons."

Keeping the Behavior Going

"At the same time," the speaker continued, "his excitement, enthusiasm, and success might be just enough to maintain *his efforts* for an equal length of time. This is, perhaps, your ultimate goal—the introduction or rekindling of the fun of learning, exploring, and investigating. The reinforcement from accomplishment, from solving, or just from doing, when it is experienced, can be the most potent motivator available to students. The problem that you and I are often faced with is how to set the stage for the student to experience this type of reinforcement. As you know, in many instances, this problem does not occur. Some students already enjoy learning for its own sake. But for those who do not find themselves in such a favorable position, our assistance can be very helpful. We have already looked at several things that can be done: the present performance level, the introduction of material at that measured level, the consistent and continuous reinforcement for all initial effort and performance. Now we need to do something else. Once the student begins to work diligently, you and I gradually begin to reduce the amount of reinforcement we give him for his efforts."

"Ironically," the speaker continued, "once our students start working hard, it is best that we do not reinforce them all the time. You see, one of the things that teachers are interested in accomplishing is helping students learn to work on their own, and often for fairly long periods of time. One way to accomplish this is to show that reinforcement will not always come; that not everything they do will be followed by praise and recognition. The outcome of this occasional reinforcement is greater persistence and perseverance. Students learn that by continuing their efforts, some form of reinforcement will come eventually."

"Isn't it true," Anne asked, "that most of our behavior is reinforced on an occasional basis? I know, for example, that not all of the things I bake come out perfect. In fact, some of my cookies are total flops. I rarely call on a student every time he raises his hand, but instead, only occasionally. I went to Las Vegas last summer and unfortunately, I must report that not all of my nickels brought me cherries. Instead, I ended up with many more lemons."

"You're right, Anne," the speaker answered. "Almost from the moment of birth, our natural environment reinforces us only occasionally."

"Well, in my case," Anne continued, "even though I do not receive reinforcement all the time, I still bake cookies, my students still raise their hands, and I suspect I will go back to Las Vegas and try again."

"What you have described appears to be the effects of unpredictable, occasional reinforcement. Whether we realize it or not, just about all of the reinforcement we use in our classroom is given on an occasional basis. Used correctly, it can be very helpful to our students."

> **KEY:** In the early stages of learning a task, reinforce every correct response. As the behavior becomes stronger, require more correct responses before reinforcing. (Becker, 1971)

From *Teaching Our Children* (Macht, 1975):

Helping Jenny to Speak

Five-year-old Jenny had very few understandable words in her vocabulary. Although many physical examinations failed to pinpoint why she was not speaking, it was the general opinion of the examining physicians that Jenny was capable of speech. A program was undertaken by a qualified speech therapist to help Jenny acquire more vocabulary.

After about six hours of talking to and playing with Jenny, the speech therapist observed the following sounds and words—good-bye, aah, poppa, mm, and oou. There was some babbling and whining, but mostly there was silence.

Jenny was very fond of pretzels. She also appeared to enjoy people talking to her, particularly when the person who was talking was very animated.

The speech therapist's records indicated that Jenny would produce about one sound every fifteen minutes. Because of this very low production, the therapist decided to reinforce any sound Jenny gave her. Initially, the therapist attempted to model sounds for Jenny. When Jenny would repeat or echo what the therapist had said, Jenny would be given a piece of pretzel and lots of animated speech by the therapist. Ten days of the approach failed to bring about much change in Jenny's vocalizations. After talking with Jenny's parents, the therapist reluctantly decided to "wait" Jenny out. The therapist and Jenny sat together in a small room, and the therapist said nothing until Jenny produced a sound. As soon as a sound was made, the therapist immediately and heavily reinforced Jenny. She gave Jenny a small piece of pretzel and she echoed back to Jenny exactly the sound that Jenny had given her. Every single sound, no matter what it was, brought Jenny a great deal of hugging and animated conversation.

Within three one-hour sessions, Jenny began to give her therapist about twenty sounds every fifteen minutes. At that point, the therapist began to wait for Jenny to give her two sounds before reinforcement was given. Jenny's vocalizations continued to increase. After one more hour, the therapist required that Jenny say three sounds before reinforcement. Within a short time, the number of sounds increased to about 200 in a fifteen-minute period.

The therapist decided to reintroduce the earlier modeling procedure. This time it was much more effective. The therapist would make a sound that Jenny had said many times. Because her procedure had changed, the therapist returned to reinforcing every correct echoed response that Jenny gave. After the echoing behavior began to occur consistently, the therapist began to require Jenny to work a little harder before reinforcement was given. Soon, the therapist began teaching Jenny how to produce different sounds. They would practice teeth and tongue positions as well as different breathing exercises. Each time a new sound was introduced, the therapist reinforced every response. Then she would begin to require Jenny to come closer to the actual sound being modeled and practiced. Once the sound was produced accurately and consistently, the therapist again began to require a little more work from Jenny.

Paul and His Attention Span

Paul's mother and his kindergarten teacher were very close friends. One evening, while having dinner together, the teacher asked Paul's mother if Paul ever stuck to a task at home. Mother indicated she didn't think so, but that she honestly never gave it much thought. The teacher related that while at school, Paul rarely concentrated on a job or activity for any length of time. Even when it came time to cut, paste, and color—things the teacher "knew" Paul liked to do—he would only work for a very short time. He would just sit in his chair until the teacher came over to him to see if there was anything wrong. According to the teacher, Paul was beginning to sit more and work less.

* * *

After several conferences with the school psychologist, a program was developed to increase Paul's attention span at home and at school. Both Mother and Paul's teacher would follow the same program as closely as possible.

Paul was given several pieces of paper, some crayons, a scissors, and some glue. Mother provided a place for him to work in the family room at home. While at school, Paul, as usual, would work at his desk along with the rest of his friends. Both Mother and the teacher would wait for Paul to begin to work with his materials. He was asked to make anything he wanted. After approximately one minute of work, Mother or Teacher would walk over to Paul. They would place one of their hands on his shoulder and briefly comment on how nice his work was. They would then walk away for a brief period of time. After another minute or so they would return to Paul, once again praising his talents. Very gradually, they began to require a few more minutes of work before going over to Paul to recognize his creative endeavors. Within three days, Paul was sitting and working about the same amount of time as the rest of the children in his class.

After seeing how effective the school psychologist's program was, Paul's teacher began to use the same idea with all of the children in her room. She made a special point to occasionally reinforce each of the children for whatever task they were doing. (Macht, 1975)

THIRTY-SECOND YOUDOIT

Carefully reread the first paragraph of Paul's scenario, up to the asterisks. Then fill in the following charts.

Teacher's Initial Program

Behavior	Environment's Reaction	Results
Desired (Paul, sitting in his chair doing his work)	Teacher's reaction—	
Undesired (Paul, sitting in his chair *not* doing his work)	Teacher's reaction—	

Your New Program

Behavior	Environment's Reaction
Desired	Teacher's reaction—
Undesired	Teacher's reaction—

Wall Street Wizards

On the advice of a colleague, Mr. Deen decided to try a different approach to the learning of addition and subtraction of fractions. He developed a present performance level test for his twenty-seven students and, based on the results, he divided his class into teams. Each member of the class was asked to bring the evening financial section of the newspaper to class the following day. In the event that a paper was not available, a student would share one with a member of his team.

After spending several days explaining the various short-hand notations and symbols, Mr. Deen asked each group to select five different stocks from the New York Stock Exchange listings. He then provided each team with poster paper and a black felt-tip pen. The teams were asked to write the names of their chosen stocks on the left side of the paper and the days of the week (for two weeks) running from left to right across the paper. Each day, the students would keep a record of their stocks' highs, lows, closing figures, and net changes, if any.

During the first few minutes of each class, Mr. Deen would either introduce or review a rule regarding fractional work. Afterward, the teams would chart the daily progress of the stocks. When completed, Mr. Deen would begin to ask different members of the teams questions about the gains or losses that were charted. Almost without exception, the questions covered the rule that had just been discussed by the teacher. In addition, he made certain that the questions were comparable to those that were either answered correctly or nearly answered correctly on the present performance test taken by the student to whom he was talking.

Initially, he would socially reinforce every correct answer to a problem he would make up from the financial section. Fairly soon, however, he began to direct two or three questions to the student, withholding his warm approval until the two or three questions were answered correctly.

He was extremely pleased with the enthusiasm the students showed toward their work. The atmosphere was exciting as the students charted their stocks. He found that the reinforcement the students received from working with the fractional gains and losses, from the team competition regarding which stocks gained the most, was more then enough to maintain their interest and inquisitiveness about how fractions are used on an everyday basis.

"I never realized that gradually reducing reinforcement would actually help a student to work harder. I always thought it was the other way around; that you had to keep giving him more and more if you wanted him to persist," Miss Martin said.

"The research is quite clear," the speaker answered. "Occasional reinforcement can increase effort considerably. But please understand," he continued, "that helping a student become persistent at a task does not guarantee that he will learn to enjoy it. There is a better chance that he will see that it can be fun to learn math and history if we can get him involved. Relevant history, applied math, and exciting reading material, coupled with occasional reinforcement from his teacher, might be just the approach to increase his enthusiasm and excitement. Once the ball starts rolling, his experienced success and enjoyment will continue, and the teacher will be able to spend more time making her subject matter relevant, practical, and exciting."

A Teacher's Reinforcer

"We have spent a great portion of our time together talking about the importance of increasing and maintaining desirable student behavior," the speaker began as he again sat down at the front of the stage. "However, we haven't talked much about your behavior; specifically, the maintenance of your desirable behavior. Your attitude and behavior is critical and anything that can be done to maintain your interest and motivation in your work will certainly be worthwhile. With this latter point in mind, I would like to ask you all a question. What are some of the things that help sustain your interest and effort?"

"I see two major things," a young man volunteered. "This is only my first year of teaching, so maybe I will experience others in the future. First, as naive as it sounds, is my colleagues' signs of approval and recognition. It really makes me feel good when one of my friends tells me that I am doing a good job. I don't know why, but that brief statement of appreciation makes me want to work harder, and my students sense that."

"The second thing is a sense of fulfillment, of accomplishment. I'm not certain how else to say it. Knowing that I had a very small part of a youngster's growth and change, and seeing him become more aware of things and try new things is equally pleasurable."

"I think most of us would agree that those two ideas are very important," the speaker commented. "I'd like to stay with your last statement for just a moment," he added.

"Along with all the positive aspects of the teaching profession, it has one potential drawback. Unless we make a special effort, we rarely know how well we are doing. It is sometimes very difficult to know if we are having a positive influence on our students. If you remember, we talked about this in the very beginning of our discussion—the idea of the observable end-product. Perhaps one of the strongest motivators available to us is the change and growth we *see* take place with our students. Their progress may be our major source of sustenance. Just a minute or two ago we talked about a way that enables us to continually see the change, growth, and progress taking place. Do you remember?"

"I'd like to respond if I may," Miss Martin said. "I am embarrassed about my earlier tirades. I must admit I was objecting more from ignorance than anything else. These last couple of hours have had an appreciable effect on my thoughts."

"I think you are referring to the present performance level and the small steps. By setting up individual programs we can watch each student progress through his own small steps. We can say that growth is occurring as each step is mastered. If we keep fairly careful records, the student can also see his own progress. I would imagine this would be a source of reinforcement for him, as well."

"Thank you, Kathy, that is exactly right. There does appear to be a strong component of reinforcement when watching progress being made. As you have indicated, careful records can make the observation much easier. Understand, however, that we are not talking about records such as report cards. They tell us very little, for two reasons: first, because they are given very infrequently; second, because they only report letter or number grades, and it is difficult to interpret what the letter grade actually stands for. The type of records that should be kept are daily or weekly records that show how much progress a youngster is making *beyond his* measured present performance level. These types of records offer a tremendous advantage for the teacher, as he can easily see how well he and his students are doing. He gives himself a chance to experience a great source of satisfaction when his students are doing well, and I assure you that he will communicate this feeling to his students. If, on the other hand, a student is not doing well, the teacher will immediately know that something needs to be done. Notice the advantage these types of records offer a student's parents. No longer will they have to wait six weeks to be pleased or shocked."

"It seems to me," Miss Martin added, "that keeping a record of how a student is doing in comparison to his *own* present performance level will also have an effect on the competition *between* students."

"It will," the speaker responded. "And the effect can be very positive. The student competes with himself. He is no longer put in a position of having to compete against someone who is much more *experienced*. His success depends on his *own* work and not on how he compares with thirty other youngsters in his class. Let me show you something," the speaker added as he hurried to the blackboard. "Suppose a student (student A) comes in to your class at a lower academic level than the rest of his fellow students. We'll say that he comes in at level two. Let's also say that another youngster (student B) comes into the class at level six."

<pre>
        Teacher's   Teacher's
          Goal   Goal
          ────   ────
          10   10
           9   9
           8   8
           7   7
           6   PPL ─────────► 6
           5   5
           4   4
           3   3
PPL ───────► 2   2
           1   1
      (Student A)   (Student B)
</pre>

"At the end of a six-week grading period, student B has done very little work, although managing to move to level seven. On the other hand, student A has worked his duff off and has progressed to level five."

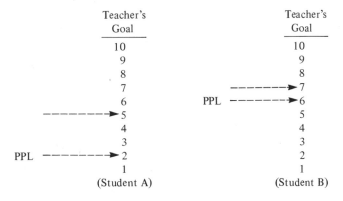

<pre>
        Teacher's   Teacher's
          Goal   Goal
          ────   ────
          10   10
           9   9
           8   8
           7   ───────► 7
           6   PPL ───────► 6
    ───────► 5   5
           4   4
           3   3
PPL ───────► 2   2
           1   1
      (Student A)   (Student B)
</pre>

"Assuming that each step is equally difficult, who has progressed more? Yet, who will probably receive the better grade? I am not saying that student B should be penalized for his 'limited' growth, but I am saying that student A's progress must be recognized. Notice that if instead of reporting progress to the student's parents, we report only grades of A for student B and C for student A, we will not be reporting what actually happened. There is, of course, another possibility. Student A might 'earn' something lower than a C if everyone in the class is at level seven or above by the conclusion of some arbitrary time period."

"Keeping records of progress beyond present performance level can show us so much that might otherwise be lost if we fail to keep track of what a student is really doing. By looking at a student's progress, teachers can 'cue' themselves to respond appropriately when certain gains or behaviors occur. When you see that your program is working, you will feel beautiful."

Epilogue

If it is true, as many hope it is, that education is the key to helping man to understand and coexist better with himself and his neighbor, then understand *your* immense importance. What you do with our children will affect us all. You do have an influence on what will be. You are no small part of the future. Look at the numbers who will be touched by you, by your thoughts, attitudes, and priorities. Look at the numbers who will hear what you say, model what you do, feel and think as you suggest.

Now, look at yourself.

Look at your thoughts, attitudes, and words. What will they mean to our children?

Look at your priorities.

Look at your actions.

Look at how the children look at you.

Look at what you will do with, for, and to our children.

You do have an influence on what will be.

You are no small part of the future.

Suggested Answers to Youdoits

You will not find answers to each of the thirty-two youdoits. Some can only be answered by yourself. The fifth one, for example, will require your own definition of the two terms. When appropriate, however, I will offer you some ideas for an acceptable answer. You should feel free to disagree with my suggestions. When such a situation arises, I ask you to do only one thing. Ask your professor for time to present your ideas and rationale.

One final point. Some of the answers to the youdoits will make more sense after you read the entire book. I believe you will find it very helpful to do the youdoits twice; first, as you come to them and second, when you have completed the book. This, of course, lends itself to a thiry-third youdoit—the comparison of your "before" and "after" answers.

NINTH YOUDOIT

Teacher's goal: To have each child complete one page of their workbook during the allotted class time.

The first three questions will probably have similar answers. The teacher's major mistake was that of assuming the reinforcing and punishing properties of selected activities without watching the effects those activities had on the students' behavior. If, as she said, gold stars and going to the library were reinforcers and, if sitting in the hallway and missing library periods were forms of punishment, then one would expect that most, if not all, of the students would be doing their math work and not sitting in the hallway. Apparently, this did not happen, at least after the program was in effect for several weeks. What was ultimately the most potent reinforcer based on the students' behavior was the opportunity *to sit* in the hallway. Interestingly, the easiest way her students could do this was by not doing their work—somewhat opposite of the teacher's goal.

Notice, however, that for the first three days of her program, things were going smoothly. This might mean that for a while, the gold stars and library privileges were somewhat reinforcing, as the teacher assumed. If they were initially reinforcing, why did this change?

One possible explanation might be that the novelty of receiving stars and going to the library wore off. At first, it was fun to accumulate stars, but after a while the fun diminished. Had the teacher allowed her students to exchange the stars for a more desired activity, one of their choice if possible, the stars probably would have maintained their potency. The same could be said for the trips to the library. It may have been fun to go initially, but if nothing interesting and enjoyable was provided while in the library, then it, too, could lose its positive quality and thus no longer be valued by the students.

There is another possibility that you might have considered. The workbook could have been boring or difficult. If the latter was the case, regardless of what reinforcement was provided, the youngsters might not have been able to complete the work to the teacher's satisfaction. Therefore, they ended up in the hallway, not because they wanted to, but because they had little option. This possibility leads us to the fourth question of this youdoit.

What was glaringly wrong was that she may have been asking her students to do something for which their prior experience had failed to prepare them. She apparently was assuming that *all* the students had the same prerequisite skills, and that they *all* worked at the same speed. She had failed to individualize her program. The fact that she made this mistake resulted in little chance that all the students would gain what the teacher had offered. This, in turn, may have accounted for the two "mavericks." The teacher's "blanket" approach just about guaranteed that some students would lose out, even if they did not want to. If they knew that they would not succeed despite their efforts, then they would stop trying. (If you have finished the section on the present performance level, I am certain you recognized the danger of the "blanket" approach. If you haven't, then come back to this question once the section has been read.)

TWELFTH YOUDOIT

Teacher's goal: To have Billy remain in his seat when asked to do so.

1. a. To have Billy remain in his seat when asked to do so.
2. a. To have Billy walk around the room, occasionally disturbing the other children who were working.
3. a. The undesired behavior. The teacher reminded Billy about four times each hour to sit in his seat and not to bother his classmates.
4. a. Again, the undesired behavior.
5. a. No way!
6. a. Yes
   b. Anything a youngster is willing to work for is, for him, a positive reinforcer. At first, he had to leave his seat before the teacher attended to him. Afterward, he had to sit in his seat to receive the teacher's attention. Both behaviors increased as a result of the teacher's attention. (You might wish to take a quick look at the technical definition of a positive reinforcer. Note that any reaction that follows a behavior and results in an increase in that behavior is a positive reinforcer. As is apparent, the teacher's attention fits the technical definition of a reinforcer, as well.)

Question: What did Miss McCawley do?
   a. She changed *when* she responded to Billy. Since her attention was a reinforcer, whichever behavior occurred immediately before it would be the behavior most likely to increase.

FIFTEENTH YOUDOIT

Teacher's Initial Program		
Desired behavior (Independent work)	Teacher's reaction— Very little attention; very little reinforcement	Results Few occurrences of independent work

Teacher's Initial Program

Undesired behavior (Requiring much assistance)	Teacher's reaction – Almost constant help; being reminded many times that he must learn to work on his own	Results Almost constant requesting of assistance

Teacher's New Program

Desired behavior (Independent work)	Teacher's reaction – Praise and attention for independent work; recognition for the *slightest* amount of Dicky's working on his own	
Undesired behavior (Requiring much assistance)	Teacher's reaction – Once instructions have been given and the teacher is reasonably assured that Dicky knows what to do and how to do it, he is to receive very little assistance. Attention should be withheld until Dicky works for a short while (a minute or two) on his own	

SIXTEENTH YOUDOIT

Dotty's moving away.

a. Dotty received more attention when she was away from the group than when she was in it. The teacher, therefore, was accidentally maintaining the very behavior she wanted to reduce. To conclude that something is wrong with the youngster's attention span is an example of how we incorrectly place responsibility for behavior *inside* the youngster. If the teacher had looked at her own behavior, how she was reacting to Dotty, and when she was responding to the youngster, it is doubtful that she would have concluded that Dotty's attention span was responsible for her moving from the group.

(Dotty's teacher's approach to group activities is quite common and it often sets the stage for precisely what happened with Dotty. Did you ever have a teacher who walked around the room asking questions from a book, and you knew which question was going to be asked of you because of the seating arrangement? All you had to do was to count the number of students "in front" of you, then count the same number of questions in the book, and you knew which question would be yours. You may have had to wait twenty minutes for your turn. You may not have paid much attention for the first nineteen of those twenty minutes. If you desired some recognition from your teacher during those "wasted" minutes, there is a good chance that you found several means of gaining that recognition. Dotty's teacher could have avoided the above situation by not going around the semicircle in a predictable way. Had she started in the middle, jumped around a little, come back to a student almost immediately after he had answered a question, she could have eliminated the wasted time and maintained the attention of her students for the total period of her presentation or exercise.)

SEVENTEENTH YOUDOIT

Mrs. Cole has a problem.

1. a. Being sent to the learning center immediately after the disrup-
        tiveness appeared to be increasing the frequency of the disturb-
        ing behavior. Additionally, many of the other students seemed to
        be modeling the disruptiveness, perhaps in order to be sent to
        the center.
2. a. Again, being disruptive.
3. a. Increase, or continue to occur at a high frequency.
4. a. Since the youngsters appeared to enjoy going to the center, why
        not continue to provide that opportunity for them? But instead
        of sending them there after they have been "disruptive," allow
        them to go after they have behaved in a nondisruptive,
        appropriate manner.
        Determining examples of nondisruptive, appropriate behavior is
        a question that must be dealt with. Once the teacher determines
        what these behaviors are, then she has developed her behavior
        pairs. The next thing she should do is to have some straight-
        forward conversation with her students. Explain to them what
        the behavior pairs are. Indicate that when they have demon-

strated the desired side of the pair, they will have access to the center. Indicate further that they will lose the center's privileges if they continue to be disruptive. Finally, and perhaps most important, the teacher needs to look carefully at what she is expecting the students to do while in class, specifically the subject matter on which the students are working. There is a good chance that if her subject matter is exciting and challenging and that if the students are experiencing success and satisfaction from their tasks, much of the disruptive behavior will reduce itself.

TWENTIETH YOUDOIT

Sharing instead of pushing.

1. a. We know that in order to teach a youngster to share, it is best to reinforce him *while* he is sharing. Removing the youngster from the supplies, as the teacher did, actually reduces the chances that the youngster will be able to share, since he has no supplies in front of him. As an alternative, the teacher might have simply removed the one object that was obtained by pushing instead of by removing access to all supplies. On the other hand, if after trying your suggestions (hopefully written for your following answer), the youngster continued to push, then removal of all supplies for a brief period of time might bring about a reduction of the pushing. For that approach to work, however, the teacher must wait for the crying and whining to cease for several minutes before returning the youngster to his chair and to the supplies.

2. a. As suggested in number one, I would immediately remove the desired object for several minutes and then I would return it when I observed the youngster sharing some other article. I would not remove him from all supplies unless he continued to push, despite the "reinforcement" for not sharing. The loss and reinstatement of supplies would depend on the youngster's pushing and sharing.

3. a. In the hope that teacher attention is a strong reinforcer, I would immediately praise the student the moment I observed him sharing supplies with his classmates. My social reinforcement would be very descriptive, "Thank you, Betty, for playing and working so nicely. It makes me very happy when you share."

TWENTY-FIRST YOUDOIT

Charlie's foot resting.

1. a. It certainly appears as if the behavior is annoying to Charlie's teacher.
2. a. Since the behavior could have been allowed to run its course without disturbing the other students and, since the other students paid little attention to Charlie's antics, I would say that the location requirements had been sufficiently met to allow the use of withdrawing social reinforcement to reduce the foot resting behavior.
3. a. The fact that the foot resting continued to occur and increase over a reasonably short time period suggests strongly that the teacher's reactions were reinforcing to Charlie.

Teacher's Initial Program

Desired behavior (Resting feet on the floor)	Teacher's reaction— No recognition or sign of appreciation	Results Fewer occurrences of feet on the floor
Undesired behavior (Resting feet on display table)	Teacher's reaction— Constant attention, constant reinforcement	Results Increased occurrences of feet on the display table

Your New Program

Desired behavior (Resting feet on the floor)	Your reaction— A small sign of appreciation; a simple word of thanks	
Undesired behavior (Resting feet on display table)	Your reaction— None whatsoever. Not a word, not a glance. As far as you are concerned, the behavior is *not* even occurring	

TWENTY-SECOND YOUDOIT

Charlie and his friends.

1. a. Dave, Harry, and Mike apparently did not want to miss further recess periods. To avoid the loss of the recess, they kept their feet on the floor. Since the teacher's approach resulted in the reduction of the undesired behavior, we can say that it was successful.
2. a. On the other hand, missing recess was not meaningful to Billy. Since his behavior of placing his feet on something else other than the floor did not decrease, the teacher's approach was not successful.

    (Remember, whether or not an activity is reinforcing solely depends on its observed effects on behavior. Had recess been reinforcing to Billy, he would have worked to avoid its loss. Since he didn't, it was unlikely that it was valued by him.)

TWENTY-THIRD YOUDOIT

Charlie

1. a. First, you would have to say that the teacher simply was not using punishment. Punishment results in a decrease in behavior. Sending Charlie to Mr. Farnum's office appeared to be the opposite of punishment. Charlie appeared to be affected by the teacher's reaction, since it continued to maintain his disruptive behavior. One might guess that the teacher's reaction was a form of positive reinforcement for Charlie.

TWENTY-FOURTH YOUDOIT

Information about Mr. Farnum.

1. a. I would want to find out what actually went on between Mr. Farnum and Charlie. Was Charlie viewing his meetings as enjoyable? Were the meetings reinforcing to Charlie? If so, that might explain why being sent to Mr. Farnum's office was *not* reducing Charlie's antics.

TWENTY-SIXTH YOUDOIT

A new program for Charlie.

New Program

Desired Behaviors	*Undesired Behaviors*
1. Keeping feet on floor.	1. Resting feet on display table (or chairs, etc.).
2. Completing work assignments.	2. Incomplete work.
3. Playing and working "nicely." No fighting or kicking.	3. Kicking or fighting

Teacher and Mr. Farnum's Reactions

Our first step will be determining what reinforcers will be most effective for helping Charlie increase the occurrences of the desired behaviors. The most potent one appeared to be the meetings he has had with Mr. Farnum. The vice-principal has agreed to help us. Therefore, along with social reinforcement, we will allow Charlie to continue his visits, but only after he has behaved appropriately.

The second step will be determining how the teacher will react to the inappropriate behaviors, if they occur.

1. Resting feet on the display table and not finishing the classwork will result in the loss of the meeting privileges with Mr. Farnum.
2. Kicking or fighting will be responded to by removing Charlie from the classroom and sending him to a location for a brief period of time where there is as little reinforcement as possible. In addition, he will not be able to see Mr. Farnum on the day he fights in class.

Once these decisions have been made, we will have a meeting with Charlie, Mr. Farnum, and the teacher. We want Charlie to know exactly what we mean by appropriate and inappropriate behaviors. Therefore we will explain our behavior pairs. We also want Charlie to realize what will happen as a result of his behavior. We will communicate very clearly what the potential consequences to his future actions will be. We want him to realize that *he* will determine how his immediate environment will respond to him, that if he desires to talk with Mr. Farnum, he knows what he must do.

Before meeting, however, we need to talk with the teacher about her class assignments. Any program that includes completion of classwork must be looked at carefully. It is not fair to request that certain work be done unless we know that the student is reasonably capable of doing it. Therefore we need a measure of Charlie's present performance level relating to the tasks he is asked to complete. If he does not possess the necessary prerequisite skills to complete the work, he will have little chance of earning his meetings with the vice-principal. That would be *our* failure. On the other hand, if the work is something that Charlie has successfully done many times, then asking him to do it again is, perhaps, equally unfair.

(There are many things that happened with Charlie that we could talk about, but two of them deserve at least a word or two. First, I hope you were a little disturbed by the teacher's statement, "Something is wrong with that boy." Based on the information I gave you, there doesn't appear to be anything wrong with Charlie. There is, however, something wrong with the way the teaching environment is responding to him. To say something is wrong with the youngster is, again, shifting responsibility, and it serves absolutely no useful purpose. As a matter of fact, it can be highly detrimental to Charlie. If we assume that something is wrong with him, we are much less inclined to look at ourselves. Why should we, we might ask? We already "know" the problem. There is that closed door. The second point is an extension of the first. Notice that Charlie was fine as long as he was with Mr. Farnum. This means that given the right conditions, the youngster was "a fine young man," and at least someone was "quite impressed with him." When we find such divergent opinions about the same student, that should tell us that the environments are different; one is more likely to set the stage for the "fine young man" than the other. We need, therefore, to look carefully at what is going on that makes the two environments, and the resulting behaviors, so different. Again, that observation should suggest that something is "wrong" with someone else, other than the youngster.)

TWENTY-SEVENTH YOUDOIT

Harvey's group.

One of the key points in this example was the fact that in Harvey's absence, the class ran smoothly. This suggested that the teacher's social reinforcement was effective with the vast majority of her students, but not potent enough to compete against the reinforcement Harvey was apparently giving his comrades. There are several ways to deal with this problem. One, Harvey could be punished for his antics. This might take the wind from his sails and set an example for the rest of the class. Punishment, in this case, would probably be the removal of some desired activity, or removing Harvey from the class when he instigates problems. Two, since Harvey seemed to be a highly regarded individual, he could be reinforced for appropriate behaviors such as giving desirable answers instead of "cute" incorrect ones, and making pertinent comments instead of "wisecracking." If Harvey could be convinced to make these types of responses, perhaps his classmates might follow his lead. Three, we could provide reinforcement for the entire class that would compete with the reinforcement provided by Harvey. Four, we could reinforce the class when they ignore Harvey, while causing them to lose some reinforcement when they pay attention to his inappropriate behavior. Or, we could combine all four ideas.

Harvey's Behavior Pairs

Desired Behavior	Undesired Behavior
1. Raising hand.	1. Calling out without raising hand.
2. Giving appropriate answers to questions.	2. "Cute" incorrect answers.
3. Comments pertinent to class discussion.	3. "Wisecracking".

Group's Behavior Pairs

1. Raising hand.	1. Calling out without raising hand.
2. Giving appropriate answers to questions.	2. "Cute" incorrect answers.
3. Comments pertinent to class discussion.	3. "Wisecracking".

Desired Behavior	*Undesired Behavior*
4. Ignoring Harvey's antics.	4. Reinforcing Harvey's antics.

Once the behavior pairs have been established, the next step might be to have a conversation with the entire class (when Harvey *is* present) with the idea of coming up with some suggestions for possible reinforcing activities. The teacher might suggest trips to a museum, special films, reading articles that compare past and present historical trends, debates in class with students taking positions that reflect different historical views, and the like. Once the reinforcers have been established, a second discussion dealing with consequences to inappropriate behaviors would be in order. Losing access to the reinforcing activities, and perhaps having to leave the room, should be sufficient to deter the inappropriate responding. If possible, the students as a group should decide what the negative sanctions will be and how they will be employed. Prior to the implementation of the total program, another meeting should be held to clearly discuss the behavior pairs and the resulting consequences to the pairs. Everyone should know precisely what will happen, given the various alternative behaviors.

Since it is possible that one or more students may be asked to leave the room as a result of their behavior, locations must be found that are as free from reinforcement as possible. If the available reinforcers in class are, indeed, potent, these locations will rarely have to be used.

The teacher is going to have to be more assertive when responding to Harvey, and to the entire group for that matter. The teacher must respond immediately with the agreed on reactions to any individual's unacceptable behavior. She must not remind the students what will happen the next time an inappropriate behavior occurs. Instead, she should immediately carry through with what has been determined.

The teacher should continue to use her social reinforcement whenever possible. She should not hesitate to reinforce Harvey for his desired behavior; if it occurs often, he will be a good model for his troups.

Despite the "usual" rule that "no one goes unless everyone goes," the teacher should not allow a student to participate in a group activity unless that student has complied with the class' rules. This must hold true even if the class is taking a field trip. Not only is it absurd to penalize all the students because of one (unless all the students are responsible for the student's behavior, which is rare!), it is self-defeating to allow the misbehaving student to enjoy the class' reinforcement even though he has failed to stick with the agreed on guidelines. In effect, this latter circumstance will nullify the guidelines, weaken the teacher's position, and point out to the other students that *their* opinions are meaningless.

Finally, the teacher must watch the effect of her program. If the wisecracking, cute answers, and so forth, decrease to a point that is acceptable, then fine. However, if the inappropriate behaviors continue to occur, then the teacher must evaluate what she is doing. She must do the following.

1. See if she is accidentally reinforcing the undesired behavior by reminding, warning, and similar comments.
2. Check the locations where the misbehaving students are asked to go. Are they receiving reinforcement (attention) from someone who is not aware of the program?
3. Evaluate the reinforcers presently available to the class. Also, evaluate the reinforcers available to the one or two students who are still misbehaving. Perhaps they can suggest activities that are especially meaningful.
4. Ask the students to help determine what problems exist. Students often notice things about a teacher's behavior of which the teacher may not be aware.

TWENTY-EIGHTH YOUDOIT

Beth.

One of the major goals the teacher had for herself was to help Beth make and keep friends. She was certain that if she could help in this respect, Beth would eventually be better behaved. Unfortunately, the teacher was unaware of the very real possibility that her reactions to Beth's behavior were accidentally making the goal almost unattainable. When the suggestion was made, in the softest of terms, that this possibility existed, the teacher was very hesitant to accept it. But because she felt so strongly about Beth, she agreed to look at her own behavior to see if it was somehow related to Beth's.

(When this "case" was being worked with, the teacher was requested to keep track of the number of times she responded to Beth when the youngster was behaving appropriately and inappropriately. After just a few days, her informal records indicated that Beth was being responded to almost exclusively when she misbehaved. In fact, the teacher realized that she had totally ignored Beth when she was working on her school material.)

The teacher was asked to determine the types of behaviors that she considered to be appropriate for her classroom. From her list, the behavior pairs were established.

Behavior Pairs

Desired Behavior

1. Raising hand when requesting help.

2. Allowing other students to speak without interrupting.

3. Working and playing "nicely" with other students.

4. Completing school work.[5]

Undesired Behavior

1. Coming up and sitting on the teacher's desk.

2. Interrupting other students when they are speaking.

3. Pushing and fighting.

The next task was to determine how the teacher would respond to the behavior pairs. In the beginning of the program, the teacher would socially reinforce Beth during every occurrence of desired behavior. This was believed to be the most important thing the teacher was going to do. It was critical that the teacher show Beth that attention would be given, but only after appropriate behavior. After looking at the behavior pairs, the teacher believed that she would be able to withhold her attention when Beth sat on the teacher's desk, but not when she would fight or verbally disrupt the class. To handle these two disruptive behaviors, the teacher came up with the following plan. Instead of using the carrel when Beth would fight in class, she would be removed from the room and taken to one of the small study rooms located in the school's library, where she would have to sit by herself. These rooms were often used to listen to records and they were fairly soundproof. Loud verbal interruptions in class would be responded to in the same manner.

[5] This one was added only to remind the teacher to respond to Beth while she was doing her work.

Realizing that this approach was quite negative, the teacher added one more component to her program. Since there was no way for her to extend recess period outside, she decided to bring a little recess inside the classroom. On Wednesday and Friday afternoons (from 2:20 to 3:00), the students would be allowed to have a free-time period in the classroom where they could talk, read, paint, play jacks or four-square. Instead of singling out Beth, the teacher announced to the entire class the availability of these two free-time periods. She indicated, however, that they would be available to only those students who did their work and behaved appropriately during regular class time. She added that infractions of the class guidelines (which were actually the behavior pairs established for Beth) would mean a loss of time from the free-time periods. She pointed out that there would be a five-minute loss for the first two infractions, and that any student who had three infractions would have to miss the entire period.

(As sometimes happens, Beth's behavior changed dramatically after the first day. The teacher was as pleasantly surprised as I was. Interestingly, there were no more requests to see the nurse, even though that was never discussed, and there was only one outburst in the library, which cost Beth five minutes of free time. Although it was difficult to determine, as a result of her behavior change, Beth seemed to be getting along better with some of her classmates. You might also be interested in a question that the teacher asked me, one that you might have thought about yourself. She asked, "How long can we expect Beth to continue behaving so nicely?" Before you read my answer, what would yours be?

My initial answer was that the behavior will last only as long as the environment (in this case the teaching environment) provides a reason for it to last. If the environment changes, there is an excellent chance Beth's behavior will also change. A new teacher, for example, might begin to reinforce other behaviors, which will set the stage for new behaviors to be learned.

My second answer was, Beth will behave in a way that ultimately brings her what she desires. If she enjoys having friends, she will behave in a way that brings her friends. If she finds out, as perhaps she has, that fighting is something that rarely brings friends, the fighting will diminish. If she finds that sharing and being pleasant and considerate and cooperative brings her friends, then those behaviors, or ways of responding to others, will occur more often. The teacher then asked, "Why didn't she find this out before? Why has she now apparently realized that fighting and friendship rarely mix?" I told her that I didn't know, but that I was willing to make a guess. It is possible that teacher attention, in this case, was so strong that the earlier behaviors it was maintaining never gave "making friends" much of a chance. Beth was reinforced for behavior incompatible with making friends. By redirecting Beth's behaviors through redirected reinforcement, the behaviors that were increased were those with which her classmates felt more comfortable which, in turn, made it easier for them to like her. That was my guess.)

THIRTY-FIRST YOUDOIT

Present performance level.

Student one:

It is apparent that we will need much more information about this student's skills before we can begin to work with him on subtraction. If you look carefully, he seems to be adding single digits more than anything else. It is not even clear whether he can presently solve "carry" problems involved in simple addition. It is also questionable whether he "understands" step eleven. It would be advisable to start him at step four. He may progress rapidly up to step nine, after which he may experience difficulty. It is obvious that this youngster is not prepared to do subtraction. Imagine what would happen if the teacher withheld reinforcement until the student successfully completed the entire present performance test.

Student two:

This student is ready for at least step eighteen. Since the present performance level test did not include this operation we do not know how he will do with "proofing." Notice, he did make one mistake (counting the sixth from the left)—the sixth problem. However, if you look at his answer to the fourteenth problem, it appears as if his mistake was due to carelessness, since he did correctly solve the 5 minus 3 component the second time it was given. Do you think he might fall asleep if we start him at level twelve?

Student three:

This youngster appears to be doing just fine with problems that do not require regrouping. Notice when he is faced with a problem requiring regrouping, he simply subtracts the smaller number from the larger number regardless of the position of the numbers. A safe place to start student number three would be at step sixteen, since the present performance level test did not provide a good sample of three digits minus three digits without regrouping. There is a good chance that he will complete that step quickly. The teacher can then begin to work on regrouping skills.

Conclusion:

The teacher should not start all three students at the same level. She needs to individualize her subtraction lessons. By doing so, she will increase the chances that each student will gain some reinforcement and, more important, experience some success.

THIRTY-SECOND YOUDOIT

Paul's Attention Span.

Teacher's Initial Program

Desired behavior
  Paul, sitting in his
  chair, doing his work
	Teacher's reaction—
	  Little, if any
	  attention or rein-
	  forcement
		Results
		  Few occurrences
		  of sitting and
		  working

Undesired behavior
  Paul, sitting in his
  chair, *not* doing his
  work
	Teacher's reaction—
	  Good deal of atten-
	  tion; teacher walks
	  over to him to see
	  what is wrong
		Results
		  Sitting more and
		  working *less*

Teacher's New Program

Desired behavior
  Sitting and working
	Teacher's reaction—
	  Good deal of atten-
	  tion; teacher will
	  walk over to him
	  on occasion and
	  praise him for his
	  efforts

Undesired behavior
  Sitting and not
  working
	Teacher's reaction—
	  Little, if any,
	  attention or rein-
	  forcement

There was a very strong possibility that Paul's teacher was accidentally maintaining the very behavior she was concerned about. Once she began reinforcing Paul's sitting *and* working instead of sitting and *not* working, his behavior changed. Even the most conscientious teacher can unknowingly develop the habit of responding most often to the behavior that is disturbing. Remember, if you see an "inappropriate" behavior frequently occurring, take a moment to check *your* behavior. The student may be doing exactly what your reinforcement is accidentally telling him to do.

Bibliography

Ackerman, J.M. *Operant Conditioning Techniques for the Classroom Teacher*. Glenview, Ill.: Scott, Foresman; 1972

Bandura, A. *Principles of Behavior Modification*. New York: Holt, Reinhart and Winston; 1969.

Becker, W. *Parents Are Teachers*. Champaign, Ill.: Research Press; 1971.

Becker, W., S. Engelmann, and D.R. Thomas. *Teaching: A Course In Applied Psychology*. Chicago: Science Research Associates; 1971.

Borton, T. *Reach Touch and Teach*. New York: McGraw-Hill, 1970.

Bushell, D. *Classroom Behavior. A Little Book for Teachers*. Englewood Cliffs, N.J.: Prentice-Hall, 1973.

Coladarci, A. "The Self-Fulfilling Hypothesis and Educational Change," *California Journal for Instructional Improvement,* October 1966, p. 146.

Macht, J. *Teaching Our Children*. New York: John Wiley, 1975.

Meacham, M., and A. Wiesen, *Changing Classroom Behavior*. New York: Index Educational Publishers, 1974.

Postman, N., and C. Weingartner, *The School Book. For People Who Want To Know What All the Hollering is About*. New York: Delacorte Press, 1973.

Premack, D. "Toward Empirical Behavior Laws: 1. Positive Reinforcement," *Psychological Review*, 1959, *66*, 219.

Reese, H., and L. Lipsitt, *Experimental Child Psychology*. New York: Academic Press, 1970.

Reich, C. *The Greening of America*. New York: Random House, 1970.

Rosenthal, R., and L. Jacobson. *Pygmalion in the Classroom*. New York: Holt, Rinehart and Winston, 1968.

Skinner, B. F. *The Technology of Teaching*. New York: Appleton-Century-Crofts, 1968.

Smith, R. M. *Teacher Diagnosis of Educational Difficulties*. Columbus, Ohio: Charles E. Merrill, 1969.

Sobel, H., and A. Salz, *The Radical Papers. Readings in Education*. New York: Harper & Row, 1972.

Stagner, R. *Psychology of Personality*. New York: McGraw-Hill, 1961.

Sulzer, B., and G.R. Mayer. *Behavior Modification Procedures for School Personnel*. Hinsdale, Ill: The Dryden Press, 1972.

Index